The Challeng [illegible] Violent Drug-Trafficking Organizations

An Assessment of Mexican Security Based on Existing RAND Research on Urban Unrest, Insurgency, and Defense-Sector Reform

---

Christopher Paul, Agnes Gereben Schaefer, Colin P. Clarke

Prepared for the Office of the Secretary of Defense

NATIONAL DEFENSE RESEARCH INSTITUTE

The research described in this report was conducted within the RAND National Defense Research Institute, a federally funded research and development center sponsored by the Office of the Secretary of Defense, the Joint Staff, the Unified Combatant Commands, the Navy, the Marine Corps, the defense agencies, and the defense Intelligence Community under Contract W74V8H-06-C-0002.

Library of Congress Cataloging-in-Publication Data is available for this publication.

ISBN 978-0-8330-5827-0

Published 2011 by the RAND Corporation
1776 Main Street, P.O. Box 2138, Santa Monica, CA 90407-2138
1200 South Hayes Street, Arlington, VA 22202-5050
4570 Fifth Avenue, Suite 600, Pittsburgh, PA 15213-2665
RAND URL: http://www.rand.org/
To order RAND documents or to obtain additional information, contact
Distribution Services: Telephone: (310) 451-7002;
Fax: (310) 451-6915; Email: order@rand.org

Preface

This monograph considers the relevance of recent and ongoing RAND research on urban instability, counterinsurgency, and defense-sector reform and provisionally applies it to contemporary security concerns about violent drug-trafficking organizations in Mexico. This research effort also involved the use of an expert elicitation exercise (using classic Delphi methods) to complete scorecard assessments of the contemporary Mexican security situation. The scorecards used in the expert elicitation were based on RAND research in the three areas that formed the thematic basis for the study: urban instability, counterinsurgency, and defense-sector reform. The expert elicitation was carried out in November and December 2010.

This research was conducted within the International Security and Defense Policy Center of the RAND National Defense Research Institute, a federally funded research and development center sponsored by the Office of the Secretary of Defense, the Joint Staff, the Unified Combatant Commands, the Navy, the Marine Corps, the defense agencies, and the defense Intelligence Community.

For more information on the RAND International Security and Defense Policy Center, see http://www.rand.org/nsrd/ndri/centers/isdp.html or contact the director (contact information is provided on the web page).

Contents

Figures and Tables

Figures

Tables

Summary

Drug-related violence has become a very serious problem in Mexico, leading to more than 30,000 deaths in the country between December 2006 and December 2010. Violent drug-trafficking organizations (VDTOs) produce, transship, and deliver into the United States tens of billions of dollars worth of narcotics annually. The activities of VDTOs are not confined to drug trafficking, but extend to numerous other criminal enterprises, including human trafficking, weapon trafficking, kidnapping, money laundering, extortion, bribery, and racketeering. Then, there is the violence: Recent incidents have included assassinations of politicians and judges, attacks on rival organizations, attacks on the police and other security forces, attacks on associated civilians (i.e., the families of members of competing groups or of government officials), and seemingly random violence against innocent bystanders.

The full scope and details of the challenges posed by VDTOs are not well understood, and optimal strategies to combat these organizations have not been identified. To contribute to the body of knowledge in this area, this monograph offers an assessment of the contemporary security situation in Mexico through the lens of existing RAND research on related issues. Specifically, we considered three strands of existing research: work on urban instability and unrest, the historical study of insurgency, and research on defense-sector reform. We extracted assessment scorecards from each of these strands of research and combined them into a single assessment tool, which we then applied to Mexico as part of an expert elicitation exercise (described in detail in Chapters Two and Three). Although none of the previous studies considered Mexico specifically, all three contribute interesting insights regarding Mexico's security situation. The goal of the current study was not to break significant new ground in understanding the dynamics of drug violence in Mexico or to offer a qualitative assessment of these dynamics, but rather to provide an empirically based platform for identifying key areas that merit further investigation.

The Expert Elicitiation

All three of the RAND studies included scorecards of factors that were used to assess a city, country, or case. To connect this previous RAND research to our study of contemporary Mexico and its struggles with VDTOs, we conducted an expert elicitation exercise based on the Delphi method (a process described in detail in Chapter Two), during which 12 expert panelists were asked to complete the scorecards developed as part of the earlier studies. The panelists engaged in iterative scoring and structured discussion anonymously via electronic media during November and December 2010. Participants included RAND staff with expertise on Mexico, RAND staff with expertise on COIN or defense-sector reform, academic and journalistic researchers who have made multiple visits to or had extended stays in Mexico, U.S. government officials with responsibilities related to Mexico, and a former Mexican government official.

It is important to keep in mind that the findings of this study reflect the perceptions of the expert panel and, as such, may reflect disagreements on matters of fact that could otherwise be settled through the inclusion of other sources of evidence.

Findings from the Three Scorecards

Once complete, the results from the expert elicitation were compared with results from the RAND research from which the three scorecards originated. We summarize these findings here.

The Urban Flashpoints Scorecard Shows That Mexican Border Cities Are Highly Vulnerable to Continued Unrest

The results of the phase of the Delphi exercise involving the RAND Urban Flashpoints project scorecard suggest that Mexico's northern border cities are *highly* vulnerable to urban unrest. This is not surprising, given that the current activities of VDTOs in these cities satisfy the working definition of unrest as used for this research. These results are based on "worst-case" assessments of Ciudad Juárez, Tijuana, and Nuevo Laredo by the expert panel and are considered to be representative of major border cities suffering significant drug-related violence.

The analysis highlights the presence of four critical factors that combine to account for much of the vulnerability to unrest in Mexico's border cities. The first is the existence of VDTOs (defined as existing rebel/terrorist/criminal groups in the scorecard). Such groups are already present, operating, and producing unrest in Ciudad Juárez, Tijuana, and Nuevo Laredo. These extant groups, along with the processes, systems, and incentives that led to their creation and to their current range of activities, must now be dealt with. Second, unmet economic expectations, coupled with high unemployment (or just underemployment), have exacerbated the problem, especially when working for or joining a VDTO appears to be one of the few viable economic alternatives for local residents. Third, Mexico is experiencing a demographic "youth bulge": A large proportion of the population is at an age that they should be joining the labor force. Many of these youths are "NINIs" (not in school and not employed) who have limited legal economic opportunities. The disproportionate rewards associated with participation in drug-related businesses also fuels recruiting to, participation in, and support for VDTOs. Fourth, deeply entrenched corruption is endemic in the Mexican government and police forces. Such corruption substantially diminishes the effectiveness of many efforts to counter VDTOs (i.e., when such efforts are not executed with appropriate zeal or when informants tip off the VDTOs regarding pending law enforcement action), and it also undermines public trust in and support for the government and police.

The Counterinsurgency Scorecard Places Mexico Between Historical Winners and Losers and Reveals That Contemporary Mexico Is Not Unlike the First Phase of Several Historical Insurgencies

The goal of this study was not to determine whether the current situation in Mexico should be categorized as an insurgency. Instead, without entering that contentious debate, the study considered the extent to which the factors currently present in Mexico make it appear similar to historical insurgencies. If Mexico were viewed as facing an insurgency (counterfactually or otherwise), how would it compare to historical insurgencies? The RAND Counterinsurgency (COIN) Scorecard assessment found that Mexican drug violence shares some characteristics with historical cases of insurgencies and that Mexican counterdrug efforts share some characteristics with historical COIN efforts around the world.

Figure S.1 shows 30 historical cases examined in an earlier RAND study, and Table S.1 positions results from the expert elicitation for contemporary Mexico among these 30 cases. The first column in the table lists the case country and name. The second column gives

Figure S.1
Historical COIN Cases, Dates, and Outcomes

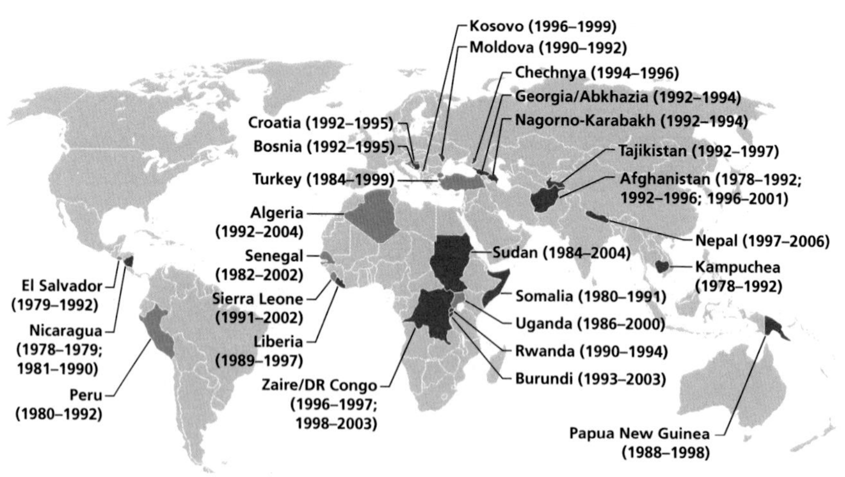

NOTE: Green shading indicates that the COIN force prevailed (or had the better of a mixed outcome), while red shading indicates that the outcome favored the insurgents (thus, a COIN loss).
RAND *MG1125-S.1*

Table S.1
Where Mexico Would Fit Among 30 Insurgencies Worldwide, 1978–2008

Case	Good Factors (of 15)	Bad Factors (of 12)	Good – Bad Factors	Outcome
Afghanistan (post-Soviet)	0	10	–10	Loss
Somalia	1	10	–9	Loss
Chechnya I	2	10	–8	Loss
Rwanda	2	10	–8	Loss
Zaire (anti-Mobutu)	0	8	–8	Loss
Nicaragua (Somoza)	0	8	–8	Loss
Sudan (SPLA)	2	9	–7	Loss
Kosovo	1	8	–7	Loss
Afghanistan (anti-Soviet)	1	7	–6	Loss
Papua New Guinea	3	9	–6	Loss
Burundi	2	8	–6	Loss
Bosnia	1	6	–5	Loss
Moldova	2	6	–4	Loss
Georgia/Abkhazia	1	5	–4	Loss
Liberia	3	7	–4	Loss
Afghanistan (Taliban)		6	–4	Loss
Nagorno-Karabakh		4	–3	Loss
DR Congo (anti-Kabila)		4	–3	Loss
Tajikistan		5	–3	Loss
Kampuchea	1	3	–2	Loss
Nepal	3	5	–2	
Nicaragua (Contras)	4	4	0	
Mexico (VDTOs)	6	4	+2	
Croatia	8	3	+5	
Turkey (PKK)	11	5	+6	
Uganda (ADF)	8	0	+8	Win
Algeria (GIA)	9	1	+8	Win
El Salvador	12	2	+10	Win
Peru	13	2	+11	Win
Senegal	13	0	+13	Win
Sierra Leone	14	1	+13	Win

At 4, Mexico is better than the worst-scoring winner but also close to many losers.

At +2, Mexico is in the empirical gap between winners and losers over the past 30 years.

At 6, Mexico is better than any loser but worse than any winner.

the sum of the good factors or practices present in the decisive phase of the case, factors previously identified by RAND as contributing to positive COIN outcomes. The third column gives the sum of the bad factors or practices present in the decisive phase of the case, factors previously identified by RAND as correlated with poor COIN outcomes. The fourth column presents the sum of good minus bad factors and is the basis for sorting the cases in the table. The final column indicates whether the case was won or lost by the government. In previous RAND research, sums of good factors minus bad factors perfectly discriminated cases in which the government prevailed (COIN win) from cases in which the insurgents prevailed (COIN loss).

Mexico, when sorted in with the historical insurgency results, falls in the empirical gap between wins and losses. The current score of good practices in Mexico is lower than that in the lowest-scoring COIN win, but it is higher than that in any of the COIN losses. Mexico's score of bad practices is no worse than that in the worst-scoring COIN win, but it is more typical of losing cases' scores. If the violence practiced by Mexican VDTOs led to this case being characterized as an insurgency, and if the current phase were the decisive phase of the conflict, a comparison with 30 historical insurgencies places the outcome between winning and losing. Of course, whether the VDTOs should properly be characterized as insurgents remains an open question, and even if Mexico is facing an insurgency, the current phase is likely an early or intermediate phase, not the decisive phase of the conflict.

Perhaps more informative is a direct comparison between contemporary Mexico and specific phases of the historical cases. In a detailed comparison with the various phases of 30 historical insurgencies, Mexico has the most in common with (that is, the greatest number of scorecard factors matching) the first phase of several different cases. This suggests that the current struggle with the VDTOs is not unlike the first phase of several historical insurgencies, and Mexico would do well to avoid making some of the mistakes that were common in these early phases, including the historical propensity to fail to acknowledge the presence of an insurgency until it is fairly robust.

The Defense Sector Assessment Rating Tool Indicates That the Ability to Control Corruption Is Perceived as Weak, as Are Mexico's Policing Capabilities

Overall, the Delphi panel's scores on the Defense Sector Assessment Rating Tool (DSART) provide the impression that Mexico's security sector has limited capabilities to counter drug trafficking, terrorism and insurgency, and porous land and maritime borders. The scores also show that Mexico's capabilities to counter these threats are minimal but functioning at best and entirely lacking at worst.

Capabilities related to border and maritime capabilities received the lowest average score among the three security issues. The average score for all capabilities related to counternarcotics was slightly higher, while the average score for all capabilities related to counterterrorism and counterinsurgency was highest. It is important to keep in mind that the highest average score across the three security areas was "minimal but functioning."

The Delphi panel consistently ranked the capability to control corruption as the weakest capability across the three security issues and a barrier to other capabilities. The findings also indicate that the Delphi panel's impression is that some of Mexico's weakest capabilities are related to policing (e.g., the ability to police, prosecute, and incarcerate drug traffickers), the ability to maintain law and order, and the ability to integrate military and law enforcement operational support.

The Delphi Discussion Highlights Certain Factors and Provides Mexico-Specific Context

In addition to the specific scorecard scores and associated findings, the expert elicitation produced a rich and interesting discussion of the various factors and subfactors in the scorecards and their presence, absence, or applicability to Mexico.

Some participants asserted that several of the scorecard factors do not apply in Mexico or mean something different in the case of Mexico. These claims highlight interesting aspects of the Mexico-specific context. For example, the Urban Flashpoints Scorecard contains a question that asks whether the city being considered is part of a "contested homeland" or "indivisible territory." The panelists recognized that this question is aimed at ethnonationalist issues that have plagued other countries but are not present in Mexico. However, several experts made compelling arguments that territorial contestation plays a critical role in understanding the contemporary violence in Mexico, because competing VDTOs contest control of the various smuggling routes and attempt to establish "zones of impunity" against the influence of the state.

Similarly, the Urban Flashpoints Scorecard included a factor concerned with the presence of "bad-neighborhood" countries—adjacent countries that are having or recently had civil wars or were host to other armed conflicts. While none of Mexico's neighbors has experienced a war or civil war within the past five years, several panelists observed that bad-neighborhood conditions still pertain, with the neighbor to the north (the United States) providing most of the market for illegal drugs and a significant flow of weapons and neighbors to the south serving as a conduit for drugs flowing from Colombia and as a source of trained paramilitary personnel for the VDTOs.

There was disagreement in the Delphi discussion about several scorecard factors. In some cases, this disagreement highlighted real ambiguity in the current reality, rather than simply disagreement over facts or definitions among the panelists. For example, the panel was genuinely split over the extent to which citizens in the contested border regions view the government as legitimate, participate in free and fair elections, support security forces, or perceive security forces as better than the VDTOs. The discussion indicated that the answers to these questions are not clear-cut and that there are real reasons for uncertainty and real circumstantial and location-specific differences in the answers. The discussion among the panelists suggests that, at the very least, these are areas in which the Mexican government and security forces should seek to improve.

Conclusions

The findings from this research effort highlight consistencies across the three assessment scorecards and common conclusions among the expert panelists.

First, according to the expert panelists' responses on the Urban Flashpoints Scorecard, Mexican border cities are at risk for continued urban unrest, specifically the depredations of the VDTOs. Several concerning factors work in combination to sustain this form of unrest: the preexistence of the VDTOs, unmet economic expectations and high unemployment, the presence of a demographic "youth bulge," a high level of corruption in government and law enforcement, and weak rule of law.

Second, based on the COIN Scorecard, it appears that Mexico is in the empirical gap between cases won by insurgents and cases won by the government. Whether or not Mexico's struggle with the VDTOs deserves to be characterized as an insurgency, Mexico would do well to seek to adopt more of the characteristics of governments that defeated the insurgencies they faced.

Third, a detailed comparison with the various phases of 30 historical insurgencies revealed that Mexico has the most in common with the first phase of several cases. This suggests that the current struggle with the VDTOs is not unlike the first phase of several historical insurgencies and that Mexico would do well to avoid making the mistakes common to these early phases, including the failure to acknowledge the presence of an insurgency until it is fairly robust.

Fourth, according to responses on the DSART scorecard, Mexico's policing capabilities continue to be weak. The Delphi panel's impression was that some of Mexico's weakest capabilities are the ability to police, prosecute, and incarcerate drug traffickers; the ability to maintain law and order; and the ability to integrate military and law enforcement operational support. Unless Mexico's policing capabilities are strengthened, it will continue to struggle to carry out these critical functions.

Fifth, Mexico faces growing challenges in the areas of legitimacy, governance, provision of services, and positive regard for security forces in the areas contested or occupied by VDTOs. The fact that the expert panel was split on many of these issues suggests that these capabilities are not complete losses for the Mexican government but are in jeopardy. The fact that these issues came up in scorecards designed to assess vulnerability to unrest and progress against insurgency suggests that they are very important and worth seeking to improve.

Sixth, the challenges that Mexico faces from VDTOs are not Mexico's challenges alone. Both its northern and southern neighbors contribute to the problem as part of the VDTO extended economy and will be instrumental in finding and implementing durable solutions.

Finally, in all three scoring phases of the Delphi exercise and associated discussion, corruption was the single biggest (and most frequently mentioned) concern. Corruption undermines defense-sector reform, efforts to combat VDTOs, and the legitimacy and support offered to the government and security forces by Mexico's citizens. The adverse impact of corruption and the criticality of making improvements in this area cannot be overstated.

Acknowledgments

We would like to acknowledge the quality-assurance reviewers for this document, Peter Chalk at RAND and Professor George Grayson at the College of William and Mary. Their insightful comments and suggestions led to important improvements to the manuscript. Special thanks are owed to the participants in the Delphi panel, whose input is at the core of this effort. All were promised anonymity, so we cannot thank them by name, but they know who they are. We further extend our gratitude to K. Jack Riley, James Dobbins, and Michael Lostumbo in the RAND National Defense Research Institute for their support of this project. We also thank RAND colleague C. Richard Neu for his informal comments and input at several points during this research effort. Maria Falvo made an important contribution to the management and formatting of the citations herein. Finally, we thank editor Lauren Skrabala, production editor Matthew Byrd, and artist Mary Wrazen for their work in producing the final document. Errors and omissions remain the responsibility of the authors alone.

Abbreviations

AFO	Tijuana/Arellano-Felix organization
CFO	Juárez/Vicente Carillo Fuentes organization
COIN	counterinsurgency
DSART	Defense Sector Assessment Rating Tool
DTO	drug-trafficking organization
GDP	gross domestic product
IEMP-DG	ideological, economic, military, and political, plus demography and geography
NINI	not in school, not employed
VDTO	violent drug-trafficking organization

CHAPTER ONE

Introduction

Drug trafficking and drug-related violence are not new to Mexico. However, the current level of violence is. In December 2010, Mexican Attorney General Arturo Chavez announced that more than 30,000 people have been killed in drug violence in Mexico since President Felipe Calderón took office in December 2006.[1] To put that in context, during the same four-year period, approximately 43,000 civilians were killed in Iraq, a country in the late stages of a significant insurgency.[2] Areas of Northern Mexico, including the states of Chihuahua, Nuevo Leon, and Tamaulipas, have been particularly affected. The cities of Ciudad Juárez, Nuevo Laredo, and Monterrey have been at the epicenter of the violence. In 2010, more than 3,000 people were killed in Ciudad Juárez alone.[3]

Mexico's police forces are struggling to contend with the violence, often finding themselves outgunned or otherwise overmatched. Police officers have become targets of attack, and, in some towns, entire police forces have resigned. For example, the police forces quit in the town of Los Ramones after their headquarters were attacked and in the town of General Teran after two colleagues were decapitated.[4]

---

[1] "Mexico's Drug War: Number of Dead Passes 30,000," BBC News, December 16, 2010.

[2] Iraq Body Count, *Documented Civilian Deaths from Violence*, data as of March 22, 2011.

[3] "Drug Killings Make 2010 Deadliest Year for Mexico Border City," Associated Press, January 1, 2011.

[4] See "Mexico Town's Police Force After Attack: We Quit," Associated Press, November 2, 2010, and Mark Walsh, "Mexican Town's Cops Quit After Colleagues Beheaded," Associated Press, January 28, 2011.

Elsewhere, police forces and significant swaths of municipal and state governments have been co-opted.[5] The dilemma of *plata o plomo?* (silver or lead?)—accept the bribe or we'll shoot you—weighs heavily on Mexican civil servants, law enforcement officials, and security forces.[6] Even high-ranking federal officials and military personnel are not immune; in the past decade, two of Mexico's antidrug chiefs have been been arrested for taking payoffs from drug kingpins,[7] and the trafficking organization Los Zetas owes its infamous origins to assistance from corrupt former military personnel.[8]

Both domestic and foreign demand for drugs has fueled Mexico's drug violence. Mexican domestic consumption of illicit drugs has risen steadily since 2002. According to Mexico's National Council Against Addictions, the use of marijuana, cocaine, and methamphetamine increased between 2002 to 2008; over this period, marijuana use increased from 3.48 percent of the population in 2002 to 4.4 percent in 2008, cocaine from 1.23 percent to 2.5 percent, and methamphetamine from 0.08 percent to 0.5 percent.[9] Geographically, the northern states of Mexico suffer the most, "in part due to drug trafficking organizations operating along the border and often paying young dealers in product."[10] Approximately 95 percent of cocaine destined for the United States flows through Mexico from its origins in South America, and Mexico continues to be a major supplier of heroin, marijuana, and

---

5 Alfonso Reyes, "Plan Mexico? Towards an Integrated Approach in the War on Drugs," *Small Wars Journal*, September 14, 2010.

6 William Finnegan, "Silver or Lead," *New Yorker*, Vol. 86, No. 15, May 31, 2010.

7 Joel Kurtzman, "Mexico's Instability Is a Real Problem: Don't Discount the Possibility of a Failed State Next Door," *Wall Street Journal*, January 16, 2009.

8 Gregory F. Treverton, *Making Policy in the Shadow of the Future*, Santa Monica, Calif.: RAND Corporation, OP-298-RC, 2010.

9 U.S. Department of State, Bureau of International Narcotics and Law Enforcement Affairs, *2011 International Narcotics Control Strategy Report*, Vol. 1: *Drug and Chemical Control*, Washington, D.C., March 2011, p. 388.

10 U.S. Department of State, Bureau of International Narcotics and Law Enforcement Affairs, 2011, p. 388.

methamphetamine.[11] It is estimated that the annual gross revenue from the Mexican drug trade ranges from $15 billion to $30 billion in illicit drug sales in the United States.[12]

The Evolution of Mexican Drug-Trafficking Organizations

In the 1980s and early 1990s, important changes in law enforcement with regard to the drug trade had consequences for the rise of Mexico's drug-trafficking organizations (DTOs). Specifically, U.S. law enforcement thwarted the efforts of Colombian cocaine traffickers to transport their product into the United States via the Caribbean. As a result, the Colombians increasingly subcontracted the trafficking of cocaine to Mexican DTOs, and, eventually, these organizations took over cocaine trafficking routes into the United States.

When President Felipe Calderón was inaugurated in December 2006, there were four dominant DTOs: the Tijuana/Arellano-Felix organization (AFO), the Sinaloa cartel, the Juárez/Vicente Carillo Fuentes organization (CFO), and the Gulf cartel. However, the constellation of such organizations in Mexico has changed as these known larger players have broken into atomized units and new configurations. Today, seven such organizations are dominant in Mexico: the Sinaloa cartel, Tijuana/AFO, Juárez/CFO, the Beltrán Leyva organization (BLO), Los Zetas,[13] the Gulf cartel, and La Familia Michoacana.[14] These groups are waging an increasingly violent turf war over key trafficking routes and *plazas* (border crossings for trafficking drugs into the United States), ports of entry, and territory (see Figure 1.1).

---

[11] U.S. Department of State, Bureau of International Narcotics and Law Enforcement Affairs, 2011.

[12] U.S. Department of State, Bureau of International Narcotics and Law Enforcement Affairs, *2010 International Narcotics Control Strategy Report*, Vol. 1: *Drug and Chemical Control*, Washington, D.C., March 2010, p. 437.

[13] Los Zetas, former Mexican paramilitary members who were previously the Gulf cartel's enforcers, split from the group and formed a separate DTO, turning against the Gulf cartel.

[14] June S. Beittel, *Mexico's Drug Trafficking Organizations: Source and Scope of the Rising Violence*, Washington, D.C.: Congressional Research Service, January 7, 2011.

Figure 1.1
Mexican Drug-Trafficking Organizations' Areas of Influence

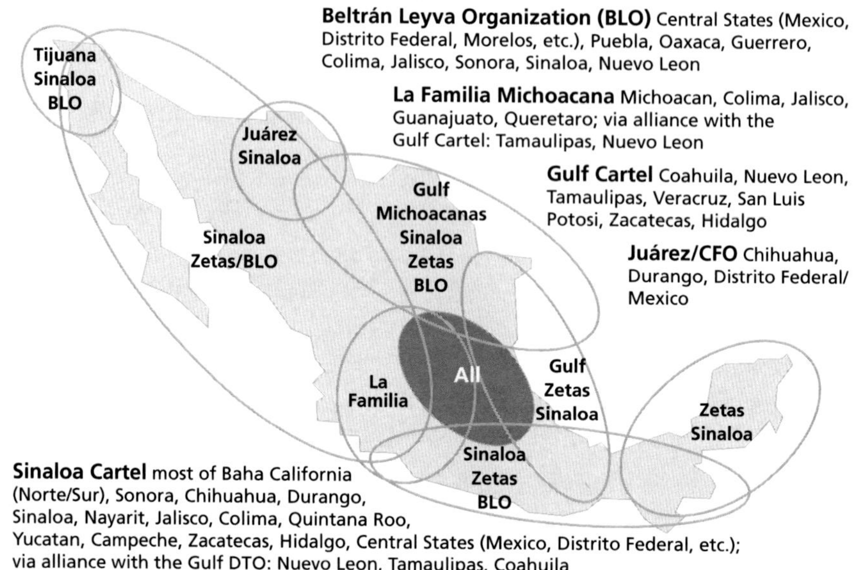

Tijuana/AFO One faction (Tijuana south to Ensenada) aligned with the BLO
Another faction (Tijuana east to Mexicali) aligned with Sinaloa

Los Zetas Nuevo Leon, Tamaulipas, Veracruz, San Luis Potosi, Tabasco, Chiapas, Oaxaca, Campeche, Quintana Roo, Yucatan; via alliance with the BLO: Guerrero, Colima, Sonora; via alliance with Juárez Cartel: Chihuahua

SOURCE: Adapted from U.S. Drug Enforcement Administration map, in Beittel, 2011, p. 7.
RAND *MG1125-1.1*

In response, President Calderón has deployed an estimated 50,000 troops since 2006.[15] On February 19, 2010, President Calderón announced that four additional battalions would be deployed to the northeast of the country.[16] In addition, in an effort to combat corruption among local police forces, President Calderón recently proposed a police reform bill that would unify municipal and state police

[15] Tracy Wilkinson and Ken Ellingwood, "Mexico's Army's Failures Hamper Drug War," *Los Angeles Times*, December 29, 2010.

[16] "Ciudad Juarez Sees 40 Killed in Violent Weekend," BBC News, February 21, 2011.

forces and place them under the command of governors.[17] Calderón has made combating organized crime one of the cornerstones of his national security agenda because organized crime is intertwined with so many of the country's other security threats, including drug trafficking, arms trafficking, smuggling, and corruption. Prospects for success in this regard remain uncertain, and the violence continues.

Origins of This Study

The security situation in Mexico is of great concern in that country and has important implications for its neighbor to the north, the United States (both a party and partner to the problem). Mexico's struggles also threaten a spillover of violence and second-order consequences for the United States.

This modest research effort sought to extend RAND's contribution to the body of literature on Mexican security and lay the groundwork for further research and analytical support. The goal of this study was not to break significant new ground in understanding the dynamics of drug violence in Mexico or to offer a definitive assessment of these dynamics, but rather to provide an empirically based platform for identifying key areas that are worthy of further investigation. The originating question for this effort, then, was, *What insights can be drawn for contemporary Mexican security from existing RAND research?*

RAND has a rich tradition of conducting security- and defense-related research, as well as research on drug policy, governance, and civil rights; these past efforts often focused on policies and experiences relevant to the United States, but also emphasize international issues, including European policies and case studies from around the world.

This study considered the applicability and implications of three specific strands of previous RAND research and related tools for contemporary Mexico:

---

[17] Randal C. Archibald, "Mexican Leader Pushes Police Overhaul," *New York Times*, October 7, 2010.

- research on urban unrest and instability
- research on countering insurgencies
- research on defense-sector reform.

The following sections discuss the grounds for the possible relevance of the prior research and presents pertinent findings from each study.

Urban Unrest and Instability

Policymakers clamor for early warning of crises abroad. When international instability is successfully anticipated, it is possible to institute some type of prophylactic intervention or make other preparations for crisis response, ultimately leading to better outcomes. In fiscal years 2007 and 2008, a team of RAND researchers conducted research on "urban flashpoints," seeking to identify correlates of and risk factors for large-scale urban unrest.[18]

Drug-related violence in some Mexican cities already fits within some definitions of unrest; whether or not it currently crosses the threshold for large-scale unrest is an open question. Applying this existing research to Mexico gives us a better idea about the prospects for the future continuation of such unrest, prospects for increases in its intensity, and, perhaps, insight into the likelihood that other forms of unrest will manifest.

The RAND flashpoints team began by identifying and collecting possible causes, correlates, and factors contributing to vulnerability to unrest. This broad-based factor identification process considered factors from the following sources:

- the literatures on various forms of unrest
- research on war, civil war, and other types of conflict

[18] For the purposes of this research, *unrest* refers to people engaged in a range of activities in defiance of or in resistance to established authority, convention, or government. This definition allows consideration of a very wide range of activities and includes (but is not limited to) everything from hunger strikes, protest marches, and peaceful demonstrations to riots, armed clashes, coups, and civil wars. We define large-scale unrest as unrest that is consequential in its effects at the national or supranational level. Because the implications of different forms of unrest vary by cultural context, we have chosen to scale unrest relative to consequentiality.

- theories of political and social change
- team members' practical experiences
- accounts of historical cases reviewed by the project team.

This process generated a considerable list of candidate factors. The list included elements that might exert a *negative* influence on the likelihood of unrest, such as mature democratic governance and the presence of peacekeeping forces. Such factors are flagged as "retardant" in this analysis.

Beginning with a lengthy "maximum" list of candidate factors (approximately 125), the project's principal investigators put the factors through a winnowing process to reduce them to a manageable number.[19] The final RAND urban flashpoints model contains 35 factors.

The 35 factors were categorized, organized, and presented according to the "sources of social power" identified by historical sociologist Michael Mann.[20] Mann recognizes four sources of social power that "fundamentally determine the structures of societies" and, thus, history.[21] They are ideological power, economic power, military power, and political power: IEMP. The RAND team added "D" and "G" to the IEMP framework: demography and geography.[22] As a capstone to the urban flashpoints effort, the 35 factors correlated with urban unrest were weighted by an expert panel.

---

[19] The winnowing process is described in greater detail in Christopher Paul, Russell W. Glenn, Beth Grill, Megan P. McKernan, Barbara Raymond, Matt Stafford, and Horacio R. Trujillo, "Identifying Urban Flashpoints: A Delphi Derived Model for Scoring Cities' Vulnerability to Large Scale Unrest," *Studies in Conflict and Terrorism*, Vol. 31, No. 11, 2008. This article provides weights for 45 factors identified in the first year of the project. The factors and weights were refined in the second year of the project, leaving 35 factors. These 35 factors and weights formed the basis for this portion of the current research effort. Supporting documentation can be found in unpublished RAND research by Christopher Paul and Russell W. Glenn (available upon request).

[20] Michael Mann, *The Sources of Social Power*, Vol. 2: *The Rise of Classes and Nation-States, 1760–1914,* Cambridge, UK: Cambridge University Press, 1993.

[21] Mann, 1993, p. 1.

[22] The current research effort uses this same organizational framework.

To apply these findings to Mexico, we evaluated these 35 factors for three Mexican cities using an expert elicitation approach and then applied the weights generated by the urban flashpoints project. The three cities selected are exemplary of the drug-related violence in Northern Mexico (Ciudad Juárez, Tijuana, and Nuevo Laredo) and were chosen to contribute to a "worst-case" assessment. Chapter Four presents the results of this effort, along with the findings that were relevant to Mexico.

Counterinsurgency

Several scholars have suggested that the current security situation in Mexico can be characterized as a form of insurgency.[23] Secretary of State Hillary Clinton referred to the drug violence in Mexico as an insurgency in an address on September 8, 2010, likening contemporary Mexico to Colombia 20 years ago.[24] Others (including Mexican government officials) have attacked the notion of labeling the drug violence as *insurgency*, suggesting that it is not an appropriate characterization or that it makes for inappropriate analogies.[25]

The goal of this study was not to determine whether the current situation in Mexico should be categorized as an insurgency. Instead, we ask the following questions: To what extent do the factors currently present in Mexico make it appear similar to historical insurgencies? If Mexico's drug traffickers at some point should be characterized as an insurgency (and we recognize that as a premise open to debate), what can we learn from existing RAND research on counterinsurgency (COIN)?

---

[23] See, for example, John P. Sullivan and Adam Elkus, "Plazas for Profit: Mexico's Criminal Insurgency," *Small Wars Journal*, 2009, and Bob Killebrew and Jennifer Bernal, *Crime Wars: Gangs, Cartels and U.S. National Security*, Washington, D.C.: Center for New American Security, September 2010.

[24] Adam Entous and Nathan Hodge, "U.S. Sees Heightened Threat in Mexico," *Wall Street Journal*, September 10, 2010, p. A8.

[25] See for example E. Eduardo Castillo, "Mexico Decries U.S. Official's Reference to 'Form of Insurgency' by Drug Gangs," *Washington Post*, February 10, 2011, and Paul Rexton Kan and Phil Williams, "Afterword: Criminal Violence in Mexico—A Dissenting Analysis," *Small Wars and Insurgencies*, Vol. 21, No. 1, March 2010.

RAND has produced extensive research on COIN. One of the most recent such efforts is documented in the two-volume study *Victory Has a Thousand Fathers: Sources of Success in Counterinsurgency* and *Victory Has a Thousand Fathers: Detailed Counterinsurgency Case Studies*. For that study, the research team conducted detailed case studies of the 30 insurgencies begun and resolved worldwide between 1978 and 2008. Each case was divided into between two and five phases. For each phase of each case, the research team determined the presence or absence of more than 70 distinct factors, derived from the existing literature on COIN and representing 20 different approaches to COIN.

This major study reached several interesting findings, including the fact that the balance of good factors (from a list of 15) minus bad factors (from a list of 12) present in a case perfectly discriminated the 30 historical cases into those in which the government won and those in which the insurgents won.[26] Specifically, of the 30 insurgencies studied, the 22 in which the insurgents won had more bad factors than good factors present, and the eight in which the government won had more good factors than bad.

What is Mexico's current score on the scorecard of good and bad factors? What can that, or the detailed pattern of specific factors present, tell us? How does contemporary Mexico compare with the 30 previously studied cases, especially the early or intermediate phases of those cases? To find out, we used expert elicitation to complete the scorecard for contemporary Mexico and then analyzed the results in contrast to those from the *Victory Has a Thousand Fathers* study. The results of those analyses are presented in Chapter Five.

Defense-Sector Reform

Security-sector reform refers to "reform efforts directed at the institutions, processes, and forces that provide security and promote the

---

[26] See Christopher Paul, Colin P. Clarke, and Beth Grill, *Victory Has a Thousand Fathers: Sources of Success in Counterinsurgency*, Santa Monica, Calif.: RAND Corporation, MG-964-OSD, 2010b, and Christopher Paul, Colin P. Clarke, and Beth Grill, *Victory Has a Thousand Fathers: Detailed Counterinsurgency Case Studies*, Santa Monica, Calif.: RAND Corporation, MG-964/1-OSD, 2010a.

rule of law."[27] The security sector comprises a variety of subsectors, including criminal justice, integrated border management, and intelligence. One of the most important components of the security sector is the *defense sector*, which includes the uniformed military as well as the military and civilian management, accountability, and oversight systems and the mechanisms and processes that sustain them.

RAND has been involved in assessing defense-sector reform in many countries around the world, including Afghanistan, Iraq, Liberia, and Mexico.[28] In addition, RAND has developed a large body of work related to building partner militaries' defense capacities.[29] Recently, the Office of the Secretary of Defense and the Defense Security Cooperation Agency asked RAND to develop what became the Defense Sector Assessment Rating Tool (DSART) to help policymakers across the U.S. government assess the defense sector in any given country and to monitor the success of defense-sector reform programs over time.[30]

---

[27] U.S. Agency for International Development, U.S. Department of Defense, and U.S. Department of State, *Security Sector Reform*, February 2009, p. 1.

[28] See Seth G. Jones and Arturo Muñoz, *Afghanistan's Local War: Building Local Defense Forces*, Santa Monica, Calif.: RAND Corporation, MG-1002-MCIA, 2010; Olga Oliker, Keith Crane, Audra K. Grant, Terrence K. Kelly, Andrew Rathmell, and David Brannan, *U.S. Policy Options for Iraq: A Reassessment*, Santa Monica, Calif.: RAND Corporation, MG-613-AF, 2007; David C. Gompert, Olga Oliker, Brooke Stearns Lawson, Keith Crane, and K. Jack Riley, *Making Liberia Safe: Transformation of the National Security Sector*, Santa Monica, Calif.: RAND Corporation, MG-529-OSD, 2007; Agnes Gereben Schaefer, Benjamin Bahney, and K. Jack Riley, *Security in Mexico: Implications for U.S. Policy Options*, Santa Monica, Calif.: RAND Corporation, MG-876-RC, 2009.

[29] See Jennifer D. P. Moroney, Joe Hogler, Jefferson P. Marquis, Christopher Paul, John E. Peters, and Beth Grill, *Developing an Assessment Framework for U.S. Air Force Building Partnerships Programs*, Santa Monica, Calif.: RAND Corporation, MG-868-AF, 2010; Jefferson P. Marquis, Jennifer D. P. Moroney, Justin Beck, Derek Eaton, Scott Hiromoto, David R. Howell, Janet Lewis, Charlotte Lynch, Michael J. Neumann, and Cathryn Quantic Thurston, *Developing an Army Strategy for Building Partner Capacity for Stability Operations*, Santa Monica, Calif.: RAND Corporation, MG-942-A, 2010; Jennifer D. P. Moroney and Joe Hogler, with Benjamin Bahney, Kim Cragin, David R. Howell, Charlotte Lynch, and Rebecca Zimmerman, *Building Partner Capacity to Combat Weapons of Mass Destruction*, Santa Monica, Calif.: RAND Corporation, MG-783-DTRA, 2009.

[30] Agnes Gereben Schaefer, Lynn E. Davis, Ely Ratner, Molly Dunigan, Jeremiah Goulka, Heather Peterson, and K. Jack Riley, *Developing a Defense Sector Assessment Rating Tool*, Santa Monica, Calif.: RAND Corporation, TR-864-OSD, 2010.

RAND's analysis of the security situation in Mexico[31] and its development of the DSART[32] were particularly relevant to this study. The analysis of Mexico's security structure found that the lack of a cohesive security strategy has led to shifting responsibilities, the duplication of services in a number of agencies, and general instability in the country's security sector, because roles, responsibilities, and authority are not clearly defined.[33] In addition, this previous effort found that ambiguous and overlapping security responsibilities have created a gap among federal, state, and local security forces. At each of these levels, security forces are unsure of their roles and responsibilities, and, in many cases, they do not share information with one another because their relationships are contentious.[34]

Mexico's security sector is facing unprecedented challenges from violent DTOs (VDTOs), and these challenges have highlighted areas that could be improved. The DSART is a means by which Mexico's defense sector can be systematically assessed and its strengths and weaknesses identified. Therefore, we included the most relevant portions of the DSART in the Delphi exercise described in this monograph: (1) an assessment of counternarcotics capabilities, (2) an assessment of counterterrorism and COIN capabilities, and (3) an assessment of border and maritime security capabilities. A discussion of the DSART findings from the Delphi exercise can be found in Chapter Six.

Labelling the Perpetrators and the Implications Thereof

One of the challenges facing efforts to analyze the violence in Mexico is the very definition of the problem. Too many of the terms that could be used to characterize the problem or label the perpetrators, prior to any analysis, presuppose what the problem is and what the outcome of the analysis should be. For example, characterizing the problem as

---

[31] Schaefer, Bahney, and Riley, 2009.

[32] Schaefer, Davis, et al., 2010.

[33] Schaefer, Bahney, and Riley, 2009, pp. 15–17.

[34] Schaefer, Bahney, and Riley, 2009, pp. 18–19.

"unrest" or as an "insurgency" presupposes a range of possible solutions. This is why we are careful to note that, while we are attempting to generalize from existing RAND research on COIN, we do not presuppose that the current security situation is best described as an insurgency. This is also why the COIN scorecard is only one of the analytical approaches we employ.

The same sort of problem pertains when seeking a label to apply to the perpetrators of the violence in Mexico. A variety of different labels have been applied to these groups, including "cartels," "narcos," "narco-insurgents," and "criminal insurgents."[35] The default standard in academic and policy discussions seems to be "drug-trafficking organizations," or DTOs. However, all of these terms have potential problems, due to inaccuracy, insufficiency, or presupposing which solutions might be appropriate. "Cartels," for example, is inaccurate. These organizations do not, in fact, collude to set prices, and to the extent that they do, that is far from being their most salient characteristic. Any term that includes "insurgency" may or may not be accurate, depending on how one defines insurgency; but accurate or not, the label presupposes the kinds of approaches that would be appropriate to resolve the problem (one or more of the COIN approaches). Similarly, a label that highlights the criminal aspect of the problem (e.g., "organized crime" or "criminal organizations"), while correctly describing much of the enterprise (the vast majority of actions undertaken are illegal) presupposes the solution: Crime is fought by law enforcement. "Narcos" and "DTOs" are better terms to describe these groups in that they are accurate (they point out both the drug-trafficking nature of these organizations and the fact that they are organized) and do not presuppose who should bear responsibility for opposing them (as both the insurgency and crime labels do). However, both terms are insufficient in scope: They do not capture the wider range of activities in which these organizations engage (including drug cultivation and production, bribery, kidnapping, other forms of trafficking, and other criminal activities), but most importantly, they fail to explicitly mention the *violence*. There

---

[35] "Narcoinsurgency" appears in Entous and Hodge, 2010; "criminal insurgency" appears in Sullivan and Elkus, 2009.

are examples of DTOs elsewhere in the world (and at different historical periods in Mexico) that are much more parsimonious and discriminating in their use of violence than those in contemporary Mexico.[36]

Because we want to be as accurate as possible and provide a useful framework for the discussion of the problem without presupposing the answer, our preferred term—and the one we use throughout the remainder of this document—is *violent drug-trafficking organizations* (VDTOs). This label recognizes that the primary (though certainly not the only) undertaking of these organizations is drug trafficking, that they are organized, and that a significant and salient part of the problems they cause is a direct result of the violence they perpetrate.

Organization of This Monograph

Chapter Two is explicitly methodological and describes in greater detail the three scorecards used in previous RAND research. Chapter Two also explains the Delphi expert elicitation approach. Chapter Three describes how the approach was applied to this study and provides the raw results from the exercise. Chapters Four, Five, and Six present analyses and findings from the Urban Flashpoints, COIN, and DSART scorecard portions of the RAND Mexican Security Delphi exercise, respectively. Chapter Seven offers conclusions and suggestions for further research.

---

[36] Consider, for example, the Japanese Yakuza involved in the methamphetamine trade in Japan (see H. Richard Friman, "Drug Markets and the Selective Use of Violence," *Crime, Law, and Social Change*, Vol. 52, No. 3, 2009), the Burmese opium trade in the 1990s, and drug trafficking in Mexico prior to the mid-1990s (see Richard Snyder and Angelica Duran-Martinez, "Does Illegality Breed Violence? Drug Trafficking and State-Sponsored Protection Rackets," *Crime, Law, and Social Change*, Vol. 52, No. 3, 2009).

CHAPTER TWO

Methods and Approach: Applying Existing RAND Research Tools to Mexico

This chapter describes the three scorecards developed through the three strands of RAND research used in this study:

- the Urban Flashpoints Scorecard
- the COIN Scorecard from the *Victory Has a Thousand Fathers* series
- the DSART scorecard.

The Urban Flashpoints Scorecard

The Urban Flashpoints Scorecard provides a relative estimation of a city's vulnerability to outbreaks of urban unrest. Note that this is a tool to assess *vulnerability* to unrest, not unrest propensity.[1] It also does not seek to make predictions. This follows from the Urban Flashpoints project's central understanding of urban unrest and is why *flashpoints* is used as the metaphor to describe the process: The project's central theme follows the "spark" and "oily rags" metaphor articulated in a 2002 article by Sean P. O'Brien of the Center for Army Analysis.[2]

[1] *Vulnerability* refers to susceptibility to a set of conditions; *propensity* technically refers to the conditional probability of an event (the event, in this case, being unrest). We characterize resulting the scores as vulnerability scores rather than propensity scores because attempting to assign meaningful probabilities regarding unrest is virtually impossible.

[2] Sean P. O'Brien, "Anticipating the Good, the Bad, and the Ugly: An Early Warning Approach to Conflict and Instability Analysis," *Journal of Conflict Resolution*, Vol. 46, No. 6, December 2002.

Various factors covary to generate flammability in a city, but a spark of some kind is required to actually precipitate unrest. Highly vulnerable cities (very oily rags) need only the slightest spark to ignite them. Similarly, a sufficiently provocative spark might bring unrest to a city with comparatively low vulnerability.

The RAND Urban Flashpoints Scorecard contains 35 factors found to contribute to urban unrest.[3] An expert elicitation exercise, the second RAND Urban Flashpoints Delphi exercise, was used to identify weights for each factor. Each participant was invited to spend "100 coins" of relative weight over the 35 factors, with no minimum or maximum specified. Participants were allowed to adjust their allocations of weight in each round of the exercise but could still spend no more than 100 coins/points. The consensus weights are the group medians across all Delphi participants in the final round of scoring.

Table 2.1 presents the 35 factors in the RAND Urban Flashpoints Scorecard and the weights assigned to each factor. Factors are presented in one of six categories: ideological, economic, military, political, demographic, or geographical. Factors with [*retardant*] after their factor label are factors that decrease the likelihood of unrest. Their presence diminishes a city's vulnerability score by the negative of the associated weight.

To calculate the unrest vulnerability score for a given city, the weight of each factor present is added to the total and then the weight of each retardant factor present is subtracted. For example, if the city is deemed to be part of a contested homeland or "indivisible territory" (the first factor), its unrest vulnerability score would be increased by 3

---

[3] As described in Paul, Glenn, et al., 2008, the Urban Flashpoints project team generated a "maximum list" of factors posited to contribute to urban unrest from (1) the literature on different forms of unrest; (2) research on war, civil war, and other types of conflict; (3) theories of political and social change; (4) team members' practical experiences; and (5) accounts of specific historical cases reviewed as part of the project. Beginning with this "maximum list" of approximately 125 factors, the project's principal investigators put factors through a winnowing process to reduce them to a manageable number. Factors were excluded if they: (1) could not be measured or assessed, (2) were country-level factors without an explicit tie to the city level of analysis, (3) were largely redundant with retained factors, or (4) were largely collinear with retained factors. Finally, factors that received 0 weight in the first full iteration of the RAND Urban Flashpoints Delphi exercise were eliminated or combined with other factors.

Table 2.1
Factors and Weights from the Second RAND Urban Flashpoints Delphi Exercise

Category and Factors	Weight
Ideological	
City is part of a contested homeland or "indivisible territory"	3
Interethnic or inter–(other identity) civic associations [*retardant*]	2
Religious and/or ethnic groups constitute contentious identities	4
Discrimination/inequality on religious/ethnic lines AND diversity/ partial dominance	5
Religious extremism	3
Economic	
Negative or very low GDP growth	1
High unemployment/underemployment	4
Significant unmet expectations regarding opportunities/sharp economic reversal	5
Widespread poverty/slums	1
Recent development economics/economic reforms/austerity measures	3
"Relative bounty" [*retardant*]	2
"Maslovian floor" [*retardant*]	1
Military	
Recent history of civil war	2
Existing rebel/terrorist/insurgent groups	5
Widespread availability of weapons	2
Tradition of effective civilian control of military [*retardant*]	2
Presence of foreign troops [*retardant*]	1
Presence of foreign troops (stimulant)	3
Political	
Mature democracy [*retardant*]	3

Table 2.1—Continued

Category and Factors	Weight
Political (continued)	
Transitional or partial democracy	3
History of repression	2
Strong state: Control over the sovereign territory of the country [*retardant*]	3
Recent history of unrest	3
Existing secessionist/autonomist movement	2
Government perceived as legitimate by governed [*retardant*]	4
Regionalism, rentierism, or other group favoritism	3
Lack of voice and accountability	2
Government corruption and low rule of law	4
Deficient formalized property rights	2
Demographic	
Youth bulge (25%+ of population aged 15–24) AND other risk factors	4
Houses significant number of refugees or internally displaced persons	2
Change in ethnic balance	2
Geographical	
Bad neighborhood (neighboring country at war or civil war in past 5 years)	3
Oil or other "lootable" commodities/wealth	1
Severe famine AND/OR severe water availability crisis	3

SOURCE: Unpublished RAND research by Christopher Paul and Russell W. Glenn, based on the second iteration of the process as described in Paul, Glenn, et al., 2008.

NOTE: "Relative bounty" denotes a condition in which residents' absolute economic condition is poor but they perceive themselves as well-off relative to an index population in a neighboring country, city, or rural area. "Maslovian floor" denotes a situation in which residents are significantly preoccupied with meeting their own basic subsistence needs (the lowest levels of Maslow's traditional hierarchy of needs).

(the weight of that factor). Similarly, if the city has a tradition of effective civilian control over the military (the first retardant factor in the "military" section), its unrest score would be decreased by 2 (the weight of that factor).

The total weight for all factors is 94. Even though each participant spent 100 coins on their selected weights, a certain amount of attenuation occurs when calculating medians. The maximum possible unrest vulnerability score is 77, because some of the factors are retardant factors, reducing propensity for unrest. A city with every vulnerability factor and no retardant factors would score a perfect 77. The hypothetical minimum score is –17 and would occur if a city had no vulnerability factors present but had all the retardant factors.

In actual practice, cities with scores below 10 are considered to have *very low* vulnerability to unrest, cities with scores from 11 to 20 are considered to have *low* vulnerability to unrest, cities with scores from 21 to 30 are considered to have *moderate* vulnerability to unrest, cities with scores from 31 to 40 are considered to have *high* vulnerability to unrest, and cities with scores above 50 are considered to have *very high* vulnerability to unrest.[4]

The current research effort did not focus on any single specific city in Mexico but rather on the country's drug-related violence more generally. Such violence is indeed concentrated in a relatively small number of cities, but we did not wish to choose a single city (which is what the Urban Flashpoints Scorecard was designed for) and then claim that the results would generalize more broadly. Instead, we considered three cities in the aggregate. We conducted "worst-case" analyses for Ciudad Juárez, Tijuana, and Nuevo Laredo.[5] If a factor was deemed to be present in any of the three cities, it was considered to be present in this worst-case analysis. Conversely, for the retardant factors,

---

[4] Unpublished RAND research by Christopher Paul, Russell W. Glenn, Kimberly Colloton, Karla J. Cunningham, Patrick Gramuglia, Beth Grill, Walid Kildani, Sarah Olmstead, and Barbara Raymond.

[5] These experiences were not extrapolated to the country as a whole but were selected because of their noteworthy experiences with drug-trafficking violence. There are many other cities in Mexico that have experienced significant drug-trafficking violence, including Acapulco, Culiacán, Mazatlán, Lázaro Cárdenas, Mexico City, and Monterrey.

such a factor needed to be deemed present in all three cities before it would be considered present in this analysis. Thus, the Urban Flashpoints analysis for Mexico is not an analysis of a specific city but a worst-case analysis of vulnerability to unrest across the major border cities suffering significant drug-related violence. This analysis is presented in Chapter Four.

The Victory Has a Thousand Fathers Counterinsurgency Scorecard

The two-volume RAND study *Victory Has a Thousand Fathers: Sources of Success in Counterinsurgency* and *Victory Has a Thousand Fathers: Detailed Counterinsurgency Case Studies* used detailed case studies of the 30 insurgencies begun and completed worldwide between 1978 and 2008 to analyze correlates of success in COIN.[6] One of the core findings of that effort was that a case's score on a scorecard of 15 good factors or practices minus 12 bad factors or practices perfectly predicted case outcomes (winners and losers) in the data. Table 2.2 lists these good and bad factors.

Over the 30 cases, taking the sum of the good minus the bad reveals that cases with a good-minus-bad score of +5 or greater were always won by the government, and cases with a good-minus-bad score of 0 or lower were always won by the insurgents.[7] In other words, scores on the scorecard perfectly discriminated the historical cases into wins and losses.[8] Table 2.3 lists the 30 insurgencies that began and concluded between 1978 and 2008.[9] It also lists for each case the sum of the good factors (of a possible 15, listed in Table 2.2), the sum of

[6] Full details can be found in Paul, Clarke, and Grill, 2010a and 2010b.

[7] Full details can be found in Paul, Clarke, and Grill, 2010a and 2010b.

[8] In this analysis, "COIN win" indicates that the COIN force and government prevailed or had the better of a mixed outcome, and "COIN loss" indicates that the insurgents prevailed or had the better of a mixed outcome.

[9] For full details on case selection and the process of data collection and factor scoring for each case, see Paul, Clarke, and Grill, 2010b.

Table 2.2
Good and Bad COIN Factors and Practices

15 Good COIN Practices	12 Bad COIN Practices
The COIN force realized at least two strategic communication factors.	The COIN force used both collective punishment and escalating repression.
The COIN force reduced at least three tangible support factors.	The primary COIN force was perceived to be an external occupier.
The government realized at least two government legitimacy factors.	COIN force or government actions contributed to substantial new grievances claimed by the insurgents.
The government realized at least one democracy factor.	Militias worked at cross-purposes with the COIN force or government.
The COIN force realized at least one intelligence factor.	The COIN force resettled or removed civilian populations for population control.
The COIN force was of sufficient strength to force the insurgents to fight as guerrillas.	COIN force collateral damage was perceived by the population in the area of conflict as worse than the insurgents'.
The government/state was competent.	In the area of conflict, the COIN force was perceived as worse than the insurgents.
The COIN force avoided excessive collateral damage, disproportionate use of force, or other illegitimate applications of force.	The COIN force failed to adapt to changes in adversary strategy, operations, or tactics.
The COIN force sought to engage and establish positive relations with the population in the area of conflict.	The COIN force engaged in more coercion or intimidation than the insurgents.
Short-term investments, improvements in infrastructure or development, or property reform occurred in the area of conflict controlled or claimed by the COIN force.	The insurgent force was individually superior to the COIN force by being either more professional or better motivated.
The majority of the population in the area of conflict supported or favored the COIN force.	The COIN force or its allies relied on looting for sustainment.
The COIN force established and then expanded secure areas.	The COIN force and government had different goals or level of commitment.
The COIN force had and used uncontested air dominance.	
The COIN force provided or ensured the provision of basic services in areas that it controlled or claimed to control.	
The perception of security was created or maintained among the population in areas that the COIN force claimed to control.	

the bad factors (of a possible 12, listed in Table 2.2), the net of good-minus-bad factors, and the outcome of the case (either a government loss or a government win).[10]

To what extent do the factors currently present in Mexico make that case appear similar to any of these historical insurgency cases? If Mexico is viewed as facing an insurgency (counterfactually or otherwise), where would its scorecard score fit with the insurgencies of the past 30 years? What, if anything, would that tell us?

To answer these questions, as part of our Delphi expert elicitation, we asked the panelists to complete a modified version of the COIN scorecard for contemporary Mexico. Participants provided scores for the 54 specific factors in the scorecard, which allowed us to to calculate the 15 good and 12 bad factors/practices listed in Table 2.2 (note that it is 54 factors rather than 15 + 12 = 27 factors because some of the 15 and 12 are summary factors that rely on multiple subordinate factors to calculate).[11]

Findings from this portion of the exercise are presented in Chapter Five.

The Defense Sector Assessment Rating Tool Scorecard

Recently, RAND was asked to develop what became the Defense Sector Assessment Rating Tool (DSART) for the Office of the Secretary of Defense and the Defense Security Cooperation Agency.[12] Although the U.S. government spends billions of dollars annually on foreign assistance, and foreign assistance programs span many agencies (including the U.S. Department of State, the U.S. Agency for International Development, and the U.S. Department of Defense), there was

---

[10] Note that "loss" also includes outcomes assessed as "mixed, favoring insurgents" and "win" also includes outcomes assessed as "mixed, favoring the COIN force."

[11] An example of such a summary factor is "COIN force realized at least two strategic communication factors," the calculation of which requires scores on all seven subordinate strategic communication–related factors.

[12] Schaefer, Davis, et al., 2010.

Table 2.3
Cases and Scorecard Scores from 30 Insurgencies Worldwide, 1978–2008

Case	Good Factors (of 15)	Bad Factors (of 12)	Good – Bad Factors	Outcome
Afghanistan (post-Soviet)	0	10	–10	Loss
Somalia	1	10	–9	Loss
Chechnya I	2	10	–8	Loss
Rwanda	2	10	–8	Loss
Zaire (anti-Mobutu)	0	8	–8	Loss
Nicaragua (Somoza)	0	8	–8	Loss
Sudan (SPLA)	2	9	–7	Loss
Kosovo	1	8	–7	Loss
Afghanistan (anti-Soviet)	1	7	–6	Loss
Papua New Guinea	3	9	–6	Loss
Burundi	2	8	–6	Loss
Bosnia	1	6	–5	Loss
Moldova	2	6	–4	Loss
Georgia/Abkhazia	1	5	–4	Loss
Liberia	3	7	–4	Loss
Afghanistan (Taliban)	2	6	–4	Loss
Nagorno-Karabakh	1	4	–3	Loss
DR Congo (anti-Kabila)	1	4	–3	Loss
Tajikistan	2	5	–3	Loss
Kampuchea	1	3	–2	Loss
Nepal	3	5	–2	Loss
Nicaragua (Contras)	4	4	0	Loss
Croatia	8	3	+5	Win
Turkey (PKK)	11	5	+6	Win
Uganda (ADF)	8	0	+8	Win
Algeria (GIA)	9	1	+8	Win
El Salvador	12	2	+10	Win
Peru	13	2	+11	Win
Senegal	13	0	+13	Win
Sierra Leone	14	1	+13	Win

previously no comprehensive tool to assist policymakers in assessing the state of the defense sector in a given country, to provide them with a systematic way of determining a country's ability to achieve various security goals, or to monitor the success of defense-sector reform programs over time. RAND was asked to develop the DSART as a means to address this gap.

The DSART is designed to assess any country across the spectrum of defense-sector development—from countries that have weak or underdeveloped defense sectors to those, like Warsaw Initiative Fund/Partnership for Peace countries, that have relatively mature defense sectors. The DSART is divided into seven sections. The introductory section examines the characteristics of the defense sector in the country being assessed. This section begins with a set of open-ended questions about the military forces in the country (i.e., their role, composition, and capabilities) and then focuses on the various institutions and processes that sustain and exercise control over them (i.e., the ministry of defense and strategy, planning, and budgeting processes). The section ends with a set of open-ended questions aimed at determining the country's overall political, economic, and security environment. The aim is to provide the background and context for the subsequent assessment sections of the tool.

The introductory section of the DSART is followed by six assessments. The first assesses a country's defense institutions and processes and determines how they match up with a set of capacities that the United States views as "critical" in any defense sector. The other five assessments focus on the country's capability to respond to high-priority internal security threats: terrorism and insurgency, drug trafficking, porous land or sea borders, piracy, and instability in the aftermath of a conflict, respectively. Within each of these assessments, assessors are asked to score the "critical" functions necessary to respond to each of the specific types of security threats along the following scale:

1. *very low:* entirely lacking
2. *low:* beginning to develop
3. *neither low nor high:* minimal but functioning

4. *high:* functional but room for development
5. *very high:* strong and no major improvement needed.

In the current study, to gauge the panelists' impressions of Mexico's capability to combat terrorism and insurgency, drug trafficking, and porous land or sea borders, questions from these sections of the DSART were included in the Delphi exercise and the panelists were asked to use the same 1–5 scale described here. Table 2.4 lists the DSART assessments that were used in this study.

Chapter Six discusses the specific questions that were asked during the Delphi exercise, as well as the DSART-related findings.

The Delphi Method for Expert Elicitation

To use the three scorecards described for the analysis of contemporary Mexico, we conducted an expert elicitation exercise using the Delphi method to complete each scorecard. The Delphi method was developed at RAND in the 1960s. While the technique has been refined over the years,[13] the fundamental premise remains the same. Experts individually make assessments or provide input and then offer written justification for those assessments. These experts are then given the opportunity to privately review the justifications offered by other participants and revise their assessments based on lines of reasoning that they had failed to include in their own initial calculations and assessments. The result is a consensual set of expert assessments based on more information than any single expert would have initially considered. Because participants work in private and remain anonymous to each other, final evaluations are reached without any of the psychological pitfalls of committee work, such as "specious persuasion, the unwillingness

---

[13] See, for example, Carolyn Wong, *How Will the e-Explosion Affect How We Do Research? Phase I: The E-DEL+I Proof-of-Concept Exercise*, Santa Monica, Calif.: RAND Corporation, DB-399-RC, 2003.

Table 2.4
DSART Assessments Used in This Study

Assessment	Capabilities Assessed
Counternarcotics Capabilities	Police, prosecute, and incarcerate drug traffickers
	Maintain law and order (public safety)
	Integrate military and law-enforcement operational support
	Maintain border and coastal security
	Collect intelligence on narcotics traffickers
	Control corruption in counternarcotics operations
	Establish drug eradication and interdiction programs
	Develop rapid and mobile reaction capabilities based on real-time intelligence
	Train civilians and military forces in counternarcotics operations
	Control roadways, airspace, and waterways
Counterterrorism or Counterinsurgency Capabilities	Maintain security throughout the country
	Collect and analyze intelligence
	Provide policing and law enforcement
	Protect critical infrastructure
	Carry out military surveillance and interdiction
	Integrate strategic communication
	Hold territory and control roadways, waterways, and airspace
	Contribute to the design and delivery of an overall integrated government strategy and operations
	Control corruption in government counterterrorism and counterinsurgency operations
	Disrupt financing by terrorist or insurgent groups from within or outside the country
	Deny support to terrorist or insurgent groups from domestic populations or from outside the country

Table 2.4—Continued

Assessment	Capabilities Assessed
Border and Maritime Security Capabilities	Patrol and secure land and maritime borders
	Track people and goods entering and leaving the country
	Control corruption in border and maritime security operations
	Coordinate with neighboring states and international community on border security
	Collect intelligence and conduct border surveillance
	Train military forces on border and maritime security while border security tasks are transitioned to nonmilitary border management agency

to abandon publicly expressed opinions, and the bandwagon effect of majority opinion."[14]

A somewhat pedestrian example of a Delphi exercise demonstrates its logic. Imagine that a Delphi exercise is convened to assure triumph in a carnival game: The investigators wish to know how many peanuts are contained in a large glass pig. A panel of experts is assembled, including (among others) a physicist, a mathematician, a materials scientist, a statistician, and an expert in the history of mountebanks. Each performs his or her calculations and generates an estimate of the peanut content of the pig. Then, each is asked to justify his or her response, explaining the calculations involved. One participant might begin with the formula for the volume of an ellipsoid and then assume a volume for peanuts and proceed. Another might begin with the volume of an ellipsoid and then add a clever correction factor for the additional volume represented by the pig's feet and head. Yet another might simply use the volume of a sphere but add an innovative adjustment for the unpredictable nature of the space between peanuts as they do or do not nest well with each other. The expert on mountebanks may not be able to articulate his or her volume calculation well at all but might make two critical observations about the kinds of

[14] Bernice B. Brown, *Delphi Process: A Methodology Used for the Elicitation of Opinions of Experts,* Santa Monica, Calif.: RAND Corporation, P-3925, 1968, p. 2.

tricks that carnival operators are likely to pull to make such estimation difficult—say, inconsistent thickness of the glass of the pig or using peanuts of different sizes. As the experts review the justifications and calculations made by the others, they may recognize factors that they failed to include in their own calculations or come to understand that they have over- or underestimated some critical quantity. The revised estimates are likely to be based on more complex calculations, be better calculations, and be closer to each other than were the initial individual expert estimates.

The next chapter describes the details of the implementation of the RAND Mexican Security Delphi exercise and the results thereof.

CHAPTER THREE

Results from the RAND Mexican Security Delphi Exercise

The RAND Mexican Security Delphi Exercise Process

The RAND Mexican Security Delphi exercise was an iterative Delphi exercise based on the classic model. It was completed via iterative email exchange between November 19 and December 22, 2010. The first section of this chapter details the process used.

By definition, an expert elicitation is only as good as the experts elicited. An initial list of candidate participants was generated in consultation with senior RAND managers and RAND colleagues involved in research on Mexico and by considering authors of recent books, reports, studies, and articles on Mexican security issues. An initial list of 29 candidates emerged from this process. Of these 29, 14 initially agreed to participate and completed the first round of the exercise. Twelve of them completed the entire exercise, with two participants withdrawing due to unanticipated time constraints. Participants included RAND staff with expertise on Mexico, RAND staff with expertise on COIN or defense sector reform, academic and journalistic researchers who have made multiple visits to or had extended stays in Mexico, U.S. government officials with responsibilities related to Mexico, and a former Mexican government official.

The iterative Delphi exercise included three scoring rounds with two phases in each round, except for the last, for a total of five phases. In the first phase of each round, participants provided scores for each factor. For the first two scorecards (Urban Flashpoints and COIN), respondents indicated whether they believed each factor to be present ("1") or absent ("0") in contemporary Mexico. On the DSART scorecard, each factor was scored on a 1–5 scale, as described in Chapter Two. In the second phase of each round, participants were shown their scores relative to the mean scores of all participants. Regardless of whether it was a first or second phase, in all phases save the very first and the very last, participants were asked to justify their minority positions and contribute to the ongoing discussion about the factors.[1]

In each phase except the first (in which there was nothing to discuss) and the last (in which the discussion had concluded), participants were asked to contribute their input. In a traditional Delphi exercise, scorers are asked to justify all of their ratings/calculations in the first round. However, because this exercise included more than 100 individual factors and because all participants volunteered their time, participants were asked to provide justifications only for their minority positions, lest a great quantity of volunteered time be consumed generating justifications for positions about which the entire panel was in complete agreement. In the second phase of each round, participants whose score on a factor differed from the group mean (either lower or higher) were informed that theirs was a minority position and asked to justify it. In this way, the discussion remained focused on the contentious factors rather than being diluted with justifications of factors about which there was already significant concordance. Scores that became minority positions in subsequent rounds (due to either changed scores or movement of the mean) were flagged as newly minority positions, indicating that a new justification was required from the participant.

After responding to requests for justification of their minority positions, participants were asked to weigh in on any of the ongoing discussions of any of the factors. Space was made available for written rebuttals, counterarguments, endorsements, and so on, aimed at initial minority defenses or the ensuing discussion. No limit was placed on the volume or character of the discussion, though participants were encouraged to be concise. Instructions invited participants to refer to studies, data sets, personal experiences, or other evidence that they felt

---

[1] For the binary (0,1) scored scorecards, a minority position was any position that differed from the group mean by at least 0.4. For the 1–5 scored DSART scorecard, minority positions were those that varied by at least 0.75 from the group mean.

supported their positions or otherwise accounted for their reasoning or logic. The discussion was considerable, spanning more than 75 single-spaced pages in aggregate.

Delphi-Derived Scores for the Three Scorecards

Table 3.1 presents the average score for each factor across the 12 participants who ultimately completed the exercise for all the factors in the Urban Flashpoints Scorecard. Because the scoring was binary (0,1), the raw average can be accurately interpreted as the proportion of participants who indicated that a factor was present in their final scoring for both the Urban Flashpoints and the COIN scorecard portions. For example, for the factor "Negative or very low GDP [gross domestic product] growth," the raw average is 0.82, which indicates that 82 percent of participants indicated that the factor was present (scored it as "1") in their final scoring. Remember that this is a worst-case analysis of Ciudad Juárez, Tijuana, and Nuevo Laredo; if a factor was considered present in any city, participants were asked to score it as present. The exception was the retardant factors, which participants were asked to score as present only if they believed that such factors were present in all three cities.

Table 3.2 presents the average score for each factor across the 12 participants who ultimately completed the exercise for all the factors in the COIN scorecard. Since all factors' scores are binary (0,1) on this scorecard, means have the same interpretation as they did for the Urban Flashpoints scorecard—namely, the proportion of participants who indicated that the factor was present in their final scoring round.

Table 3.3 reports the average score for each factor across the 12 participants who ultimately completed the exercise for all the factors in the DSART Scorecard. The DSART Scorecard uses a five-point scale, so reported averages are merely average scores with no proportion interpretation available.

Findings drawn from the Delphi results for each of the three scorecards are discussed in Chapters Four through Six.

Table 3.1
Mean Delphi Scores for the Urban Flashpoints Scorecard

Category and Factors	Mean Score
Ideological	
Ciudad Juárez, Tijuana, or Nuevo Laredo is part of a contested homeland or "indivisible territory"	0.55
Ciudad Juárez, Tijuana, and Nuevo Laredo contain interethnic or inter–(other identity) civic associations [*retardant*]	0.00
Religious and/or ethnic groups constitute contentious identities	0.09
Discrimination/inequality on religious/ethnic lines AND ethnic/religious diversity or partial dominance	0.09
Religious extremism	0.18
Economic	
Negative or very low GDP growth	0.82
High unemployment/underemployment	1.00
Significant unmet expectations regarding opportunities/sharp economic reversal	0.91
Widespread poverty/slums	0.91
Recent development economics/economic reforms/austerity measures	0.09
"Relative bounty" [*retardant*]	0.00
"Maslovian floor" [*retardant*]	0.09
Military	
Recent history of civil war	0.18
Existing rebel/terrorist/criminal groups	1.00
Widespread availability of weapons	1.00
Tradition of effective civilian control of military [*retardant*]	0.45
Presence of foreign troops [*retardant*]	0.00
Presence of foreign troops (stimulant)	0.00

Table 3.1—Continued

Category and Factors	Mean Score
Political	
Mature democracy [*retardant*]	0.27
Transitional or partial democracy	0.73
History of repression	0.45
Strong national government: Does the government's power extend over the sovereign territory of the country? [*retardant*]	0.09
Recent history of unrest	1.00
Existing secessionist/autonomist movement	0.09
Government perceived as legitimate by governed [*retardant*]	0.64
Regionalism, rentierism, or other group favoritism	0.73
Lack of voice and accountability	0.82
Government corruption and low rule of law	1.00
Deficient formalized property rights	0.64
Demographics	
Youth bulge (25%+ of population aged 15–24) AND other risk factors (at least one: high unemployment, significant unmet expectations, existing terrorist/criminal groups, partial/transitional democracy)	0.91
Houses significant number of refugees or internally displaced persons	0.18
Change in ethnic balance	0.00
Geographic	
Bad neighborhood (neighboring country at war or civil war in past 5 years)	0.27
Oil or other "lootable" commodities/wealth	0.82
Severe famine AND/OR severe water availability crisis	0.00

Table 3.2
Mean Delphi Scores for the Counterinsurgency Scorecard

Factor	Mean Score
Forces of order and government actions consistent with messages (delivering on promises)	0.09
Forces of order maintaining credibility with populations in the area of conflict (includes expectation management)	0.09
Messages/themes coherent with overall security approach	0.27
Forces of order avoid creating unattainable expectations	0.09
Themes and messages coordinated across all government agencies in or affecting area of conflict	0.09
Earnest information operation/psychological operation/strategic communication/messaging effort by government/forces of order	0.00
Unity of effort/unity of command of forces of order maintained	0.00
Flow of criminal support across border(s) being significantly decreased or remaining dramatically reduced or largely absent	0.00
Important external support to criminals being significantly reduced	0.00
Important internal support to criminals being significantly reduced	0.00
Criminals' ability to replenish resources being significantly diminished	0.00
Criminals unable to maintain or grow force size	0.00
Efforts by forces of order resulting in increased costs for criminal processes	0.91
Forces of order effectively disrupting criminal recruiting	0.00
Forces of order effectively disrupting criminal materiel acquisition	0.00
Forces of order effectively disrupting criminal intelligence	0.00
Forces of order effectively disrupting criminal financing	0.00
Government corruption reduced/good governance increased since onset of conflict	0.09
Government leaders selected in a manner considered just and fair by majority of population in the area of conflict	0.45
Majority of citizens view government as legitimate in the area of conflict	0.64
Government providing better governance than criminals in area of conflict	0.45

Table 3.2—Continued

Factor	Mean Score
Forces of order providing or ensuring basic services in areas they control or claim to control	0.55
Government a functional democracy	0.36
Government a partial or transitional democracy	0.64
Free and fair elections held	0.73
Government respects human rights and allows free press	0.27
Intelligence adequate to lead to capture of or engagements with criminals on the terms of the forces of order	0.27
Intelligence adequate to allow forces of order to disrupt criminal processes or operations	0.36
Forces of order of sufficient strength to force criminals to fight as guerrillas	0.64
Government/state is competent	0.73
Forces of order avoiding excessive collateral damage, disproportionate use of force, or other illegitimate applications of force	0.27
Forces of order seeking to engage and establish positive relations with population(s) in area of conflict	0.18
Short-term investments, improvements in infrastructure/development, or property reform in area of conflict	0.45
Majority of population in areas of conflict supports/favors forces of order over the criminals	0.64
Forces of order establishing and then expanding secure areas	0.09
Forces of order have and use uncontested air dominance	1.00
Perception of security being created or maintained among populations in areas of conflict	0.00
Forces of order employing escalating repression	0.27
Forces of order employing collective punishment	0.09
Primary forces of order come from outside the country	0.00
Forces of order or government actions contributing to substantial new grievances claimed by the criminals or the population	1.00

Table 3.2—Continued

Factor	Mean Score
Militias working at cross-purposes with forces of order/government	0.09
Forces of order resettling/removing civilian populations for population control	0.00
Forces of order collateral damage perceived by population in area of conflict as worse than criminals'	0.09
In area of conflict, forces of order perceived as worse than criminals	0.36
Forces of order failing to adapt to changes in adversary strategy, operations, or tactics	0.64
Forces of order engaging in more coercion/intimidation than criminals	0.00
Criminals individually superior to the forces of order by being either more professional or better motivated	0.82
Forces of order or allies rely on looting for sustainment	0.00
Forces of order and government have different goals/level of commitment	0.91

Table 3.3
Mean Delphi Scores for the Defense Sector Assessment Rating Tool Scorecard

Assessment	Capabilities Assessed	Mean Score
Counternarcotics Capabilities	Police, prosecute, and incarcerate drug traffickers	1.91
	Maintain law and order (public safety)	1.91
	Integrate military and law-enforcement operational support	1.82
	Maintain border and coastal security	2.55
	Collect intelligence on narcotics traffickers	2.36
	Control corruption in counternarcotics operations	1.27
	Establish drug eradication and interdiction programs	2.45
	Develop rapid and mobile reaction capabilities based on real-time intelligence	2.18
	Train civilians and military forces in counternarcotics operations	2.09
	Control roadways, airspace, and waterways	2.45
Counterterrorism or Counterinsurgency Capabilities	Maintain security throughout the country	2.36
	Collect and analyze intelligence	2.45
	Provide policing and law enforcement	1.91
	Protect critical infrastructure	3.18
	Carry out military surveillance and interdiction	2.45
	Integrate strategic communication	1.82
	Hold territory and control roadways, waterways, and airspace	3.00
	Contribute to the design and delivery of an overall integrated government strategy and operations	2.09
	Control corruption in government counterterrorism and counterinsurgency operations	1.64
	Disrupt financing by terrorist or insurgent groups from within or outside the country	1.82

Table 3.3—Continued

Assessment	Capabilities Assessed	Mean Score
	Deny support to terrorist or insurgent groups from domestic populations or from outside the country	1.91
Border and Maritime Security Capabilities	Patrol and secure land and maritime borders	2.36
	Track people and goods entering and leaving the country	2.18
	Control corruption in border and maritime security operations	1.45
	Coordinate with neighboring states and international community on border security	2.64
	Collect intelligence and conduct border surveillance	2.09
	Train military forces on border and maritime security while border security tasks are transitioned to nonmilitary border management agency	1.73

Delphi Discussion

The Delphi process also involves discussion among participants as they first justify their minority positions and then rebut, make rejoinder to, agree with, or discuss the views offered by others. Sometimes, this discussion is persuasive and facilitates consensus. Other times, the discussion is contentious and helps highlight very real disagreements. In the RAND Mexican Security Delphi exercise the discussion was very rich. Several factors produced highly contentious exchanges that highlighted real disagreements about the facts in some parts of the country, different understandings of the factors themselves, and disputes about the appropriateness and applicability of some of the factors in the context of contemporary Mexico. These discussions are interesting and useful beyond the context of justification and consensus-building within the confines of the exercise. Examples drawn from the discussion and an examination of contentious factors are presented in Chapters Four through Six.

CHAPTER FOUR

Findings from the Urban Flashpoints Scorecard

The Urban Flashpoints Scorecard portion of the RAND Mexican Security Delphi exercise sought to elicit worst-case analyses of Ciudad Juárez, Tijuana, and Nuevo Laredo to assess the general vulnerability to continued and future unrest of Mexican border cities currently experiencing significant drug-related violence. As noted in Chapter Two, these three cities are worst-case examples of Mexican border cities experiencing drug violence and are not broadly representative of all border cities or all Mexican cities. In others words, this is a worst-case analysis of worst-case cities.

Mexico's Urban Flashpoints Vulnerability Score

Table 3.1 in Chapter Three presented the raw average scores for the Urban Flashpoints Scorecard. The Urban Flashpoints Scorecard was not designed to accommodate fractional values; it requires a clear adjudication, present (1) or absent (0), for each flashpoint factor. To employ the Urban Flashpoints Scorecard in the way intended, we pushed the Delphi exercise means toward consensus positions, where possible. Specifically, if there was at least 70-percent consensus on a factor, the factor was rounded in the direction of consensus (so, scores of 0.7 or higher were rounded to 1, and scores of 0.3 or lower were rounded to 0). For factors without agreement from at least 70 percent of participants, the scores indicate this lack of consensus and are rounded to 0.5—neither present nor absent. The required consensus was not reached for five of the 35 flashpoint factors; all five were rounded to 0.5.

Table 4.1 presents results of applying the consensus scores from the RAND Mexican Security Delphi exercise to the Urban Flashpoints Scorecard. The first column lists the factors. The second column, under the heading "Factor Weight," presents the weights produced by the Urban Flashpoints project (previously presented in Table 2.1). The third column indicates the consensus presence or absence score under the heading "Rounded Result," scored 1 if consensus was that the factor was present, 0 if consensus was that the factor was absent, and 0.5 if consensus was lacking. These rounded results come directly from the raw averages in Table 3.1, rounded as described earlier. The fourth column indicates the contribution of that factor to the total unrest score and is the product of the factor weights and the rounded results. The fifth column shows the total contribution to the unrest vulnerability score from within each of the IEMP-DG categories, explained in Chapter Two. The last row in Table 4.1 provides the total unrest vulnerability score for Mexico: 38.5.

A score of 38.5 indicates *high* vulnerability to urban unrest, according to the general findings of the RAND Urban Flashpoints project. Two things might mitigate or modify this finding slightly. First, this phase of the expert elicitation exercise represented a worst-case analysis across three cities, so no single Mexican city is likely to be as vulnerable to unrest as this score suggests. Second, because five of the 40 factors were not subject to agreement by the Delphi panel, the score of 38.5 includes half-weights to reflect neither presence nor absence for the five factors without consensus. If these nonconsensus factors are all pushed one way or the other, the score could change by 6.5 points in either direction, resulting in a range of 32–45.

Even with these possible modifiers, the Urban Flashpoints Scorecard suggests significant vulnerability to unrest in the selected Mexican border cities, unsurprising given VDTOs' ongoing activities and their consequences.

Table 4.1
Unrest Vulnerability Score for Mexico Based on the Urban Flashpoints Scorecard Portion of the Delphi Exercise

Category and Factors	Factor Weight	Rounded Result	Unrest Score	By Category
Ideological				1.5
Ciudad Juárez, Tijuana, or Nuevo Laredo is part of a contested homeland or "indivisible territory"	3	0.5	1.5	
Ciudad Juárez, Tijuana, and Nuevo Laredo contain interethnic or inter–(other identity) civic associations [*retardant*]	–2	0	0	
Religious and/or ethnic groups constitute contentious identities	4	0	0	
Discrimination/inequality on religious/ethnic lines AND ethnic/religious diversity or partial dominance	5	0	0	
Religious extremism	3	0	0	
Economic				11
Negative or very low GDP growth	1	1	1	
High unemployment/underemployment	4	1	4	
Significant unmet expectations regarding opportunities/sharp economic reversal	5	1	5	
Widespread poverty/slums	1	1	1	
Recent development economics/economic reforms/austerity measures	3	0	0	
"Relative bounty" [*retardant*]	–2	0	0	
"Maslovian floor" [*retardant*]	–1	0	0	

Table 4.1—Continued

Category and Factors	Factor Weight	Rounded Result	Unrest Score	By Category
Military				6
Recent history of civil war	2	0	0	
Existing rebel/terrorist/criminal groups	5	1	5	
Widespread availability of weapons	2	1	2	
Tradition of effective civilian control of military [*retardant*]	–2	0.5	–1	
Presence of foreign troops (in these cities) [*retardant*]	–1	0	0	
Presence of foreign troops (stimulant in these cities)	3	0	0	
Political				15
Mature democracy [*retardant*]	–3	0	0	
Transitional or partial democracy	3	1	3	
History of repression	2	0.5	1	
Strong national government: Does the government's power extend over the sovereign territory of the country? [*retardant*]	–3	0	0	
Recent history of unrest	3	1	3	
Existing secessionist/autonomist movement	2	0	0	
Government perceived as legitimate by governed [*retardant*]	–4	0.5	–2	

Table 4.1—Continued

Category and Factors	Factor Weight	Rounded Result	Unrest Score	By Category
Political (continued)				
Regionalism, rentierism, or other group favoritism	3	1	3	
Lack of voice and accountability	2	1	2	
Government corruption and low rule of law	4	1	4	
Deficient formalized property rights	2	0.5	1	
Demographics				4
Youth bulge (25%+ of population aged 15–24) AND other risk factors (at least one: high unemployment, significant unmet expectations, existing terrorist/criminal groups, partial/transitional democracy)	4	1	4	
Houses significant refugees or internally displaced persons	2	0	0	
Change in ethnic balance	2	0	0	
Geographic			**0**	1
Bad neighborhood (neighboring country at war or civil war in past 5 years)	3	0	0	
Oil or other "lootable" commodities/wealth	1	1	1	
Severe famine AND/OR severe water availability crisis	3	0	0	
Total unrest score				38.5

Flashpoint Factors of Concern in Mexico

Because the Urban Flashpoints Scorecard provides weights for individual factors, it enables the identification of factors of particular concern in addition to providing a summary score. If we consider factors with a weight of 4 or 5 (5 being the highest single weight in the scorecard) against the factors deemed present in Mexico by the Delphi panel, we get a summary of the factors that are most concerning for Mexico against the context of a generic outside perspective on urban unrest. Five factors have an unrest vulnerability weight of 4 or 5 and were deemed present in at least one of the Mexican cities considered:

- Existing rebel/terrorist/criminal groups
- High unemployment/underemployment
- Significant unmet expectations regarding opportunities/sharp economic reversal
- Youth bulge (more than 25 percent of the population aged 15–24) *and* other risk factors (at least one of the following: high unemployment, significant unmet expectations, existing terrorist/criminal groups, partial/transitional democracy)
- Government corruption and low rule of law.

Although the importance of these factors comes from broader research on urban unrest in general and was not derived in a way that was context-specific to Mexico, the factors highlighted correspond with many of the compelling narratives about the challenges Mexico faces. First, VDTOs have already been established and are successfully engaged in a host of lucrative drug-related enterprises (with a gross volume in the tens of billions of dollars),[1] as well as in signifi-

[1] Estimates of the economic magnitude of the drug trade and related activities vary widely. Robert J. Bunker, "Strategic Threat: Narcos and Narcotics Overview," *Small Wars and Insurgencies*, Vol. 21, No. 1, 2010, places the total Mexican "cartel" economy at $20 billion. Jonathan P. Caulkins, Peter Reuter, Martin Y. Iguchi, and James Chiesa, *How Goes the "War on Drugs"? An Assessment of U.S. Drug Problems and Policy*, Santa Monica, Calif.: RAND Corporation, OP-121-DPRC, 2005, estimate the total U.S. drug industry (a significant fraction of the supply originates in or transits Mexico) at $60 billion. The article "Organized Crime in Mexico," *STRATFOR*, March 11, 2008, estimates that $25–$30 billion worth of illegal

cant related violence (as noted earlier, more than 30,000 people were killed between December 2006 and December 2010). Unlike groups that might come together and foment unrest in other countries, unrest is already occurring in Mexico and will continue to do so while the authorities attempt to thwart the VDTOs and their activities.

The second challenge is the combination of economic distress and a "youth bulge."[2] While unemployment and a perceived lack of economic opportunities are easily understood, when these factors accompany a youth bulge, a demographic trend in which a significant portion of the population is, or will soon be, of age to enter the workforce, this can be a toxic mix. The Urban Flashpoints Scorecard indicates that a youth bulge by itself is not an exceptional risk factor, but when it accompanies one or more of four other risk factors (high unemployment/underemployment, significant unmet economic expectations, existing rebel/terrorist/criminal groups, or transitional/partial democracy), it is an extremely volatile ingredient. The Delphi panel judged all four of these interactive risk-increasing factors to be present in Mexico, and the discussion highlighted concerns in this area. One participant explained, "The term used to describe the vulnerability of marginalized youth in Mexico is NINI (not in school and not employed)," adding that the term is in wide use to describe an acknowledged (and troublesome) problem.

The interaction of these factors, along with the presence of VDTOs, is concerning.[3] A significant youth bulge, in the presence

---

drugs enters the United States from Mexico each year, which does not account for Mexico's entire drug economy. Beau Kilmer, Jonathan P. Caulkins, Brittany M. Bond, and Peter H. Reuter, *Reducing Drug Trafficking Revenues and Violence in Mexico: Would Legalizing Marijuana in California Help?* Santa Monica, Calif.: RAND Corporation, OP-325-RC, 2010, estimated DTOs' gross revenue from traffic just for marijuana and only that entering the United States at between $1.5 and $2 billion per year.

[2] The seminal work on the links between youth bulges and violence is Jack A. Goldstone, *Revolution and Rebellion in the Early Modern World*, Berkeley, Calif.: University of California Press, 1991.

[3] If there are substantial shifts in the population from one region of the country to another due to drug violence, it could also create additional pressure on Mexico's institutions and infrastructure.

of dissatisfaction with available economic opportunities, creates an ideal mix for VDTOs to recruit and garner support.

Finally, "Government corruption and low rule of law" forms the cornerstone of many narratives about Mexican security, either as a core part of the problem, part of the difficulty of combating VDTOs, or both. The effective penetration of the government and the police by the VDTOs (silver or lead?) is a cumulative challenge from an unrest perspective. First, corruption diminishes effectiveness in general and increases dissatisfaction with the government, which decreases legitimacy and support for the government, and increases prospects for unrest. In addition, corruption diminishes the effectiveness of efforts to counter the VDTOs, allowing them to perpetuate adverse security conditions.

A reviewer pointed out that these conditions are exacerbated by the independent power of Mexico's state governors. Governors have extreme autonomy and latitude relative to the central government and have been characterized by some as the "new viceroys."[4] Governors who wish to do so can substantially divert state funds to the benefit of themselves and their cronies, and quickly spread corruption and destroy legitimacy throughout a state. Some state governors are believed to be aligned with the VDTOs, and incentives (silver or lead?) are very strong for those who do not reach some sort of accommodation or understanding with groups.

Flashpoint Factors for Which Concensus Was Lacking and Other Items of Interest from the Delphi Discussion

The Delphi panel did not reach consensus on five of the Urban Flashpoints factors:

- Ciudad Juárez, Tijuana, or Nuevo Laredo is part of a contested homeland or "indivisible territory"
- Tradition of effective civilian control of military [*retardant*]

---

[4] Leo Zuckerman, "Los Nuevos Virreyes" ["The New Viceroys"], *Proceso*, July 13, 2003.

- History of repression
- Government perceived as legitimate by governed [*retardant*]
- Deficient formalized property rights.

The discussion related to these disagreements raised many interesting points, some of which are discussed here.

Regarding these cities being part of a contested homeland, most participants appeared to agree that they are not such in the traditional sense of being contested by different ethnic or ethnonationalist groups. However, many participants asserted a very different kind of contestation and asserted its importance for understanding the current security situation. As one participant noted,

> These areas are not contested between ethnic or national groups in a conventional sense. They are fiercely contested, however, by several well-armed, ruthless criminal organizations which seek territorial dominance. Fighting for criminal control of "plazas" may not be the same thing as fighting for a "homeland," but it is certainly violence associated with competition for "contested" territory.

A reviewer pointed out that La Familia Michoacana asserts a *michoacanos* identity and publicly claims to combat the threat posed by "outsiders." Another participant passionately argued that the answer to the question, "Who is in charge in these cities?" does not have a clear answer, and that this fact argues quite strongly that these cities should be viewed as contested, "since there is no sense of anyone actually governing and demonstrating leadership worth following."

While we agree that this factor is probably not present in the way that the RAND Urban Flashpoints project team intended, the contested nature of these spaces is apparent and is clearly an important contributor to the current violence. The increased violence could be partially a result of the fragmentation of some large DTOs into smaller ones and the ensuing competition among them, as well as the government's crackdown on these groups.

While the lack of consensus on the contested homeland factor was more about the factor definition and the implications for Mexico than a disagreement regarding facts, the lack of consensus on the extent of a tradition of effective civilian control of the military was much more characterized by factual disagreement. Those supporting the presence of a tradition of civilian control pointed out the high-level of respect accorded the military in Mexico relative to the government, the police, or virtually any other institution or group. They also pointed out the lack of a military coup or other direct participation in politics (in contrast to many other countries in Central and South America). Without disputing those facts, those disagreeing that there is a tradition of civilian control argued for nuance: Just because the military hasn't overthrown the government doesn't mean that it is meaningfully under the government's control. One participant articulated this position particularly clearly:

> The Mexican military has in recent decades been held largely separate from the rest of Mexican society. While this separation has had the significant benefit of discouraging the military from taking over the state directly (as in many other parts of Latin America) this arms-length relationship does not in fact constitute civilian control of the military, as the situation is conventionally mis-characterized. In fact, the Mexican military almost completely controls what it considers to be its own internal affairs, with little civilian oversight. It is true that the Mexican military seems to be loyal institutionally to the established Mexican constitutional order, that the Mexican military is far less likely to violate civil or human rights than is the police, and that the Mexican military usually obeys direct, explicit orders from the Mexican President. That general institutional discipline is not, however, the same as effective civilian control of how the military conducts operations, organizes itself, trains personnel, etc., which would be the correct functions of a modern, democratic government with respect to its military arm.

The matter is further complicated by the frequency with which mayors and governors appoint former military officers to civilian security posts. The nuance and extent of effective civilian control over the military are probably of limited consequence over the short term. None of the Delphi participants argued that the Mexican government is under any threat from the country's military. Such differences between conditions in Mexico and what is traditionally considered effective civilian control could matter in the medium or long term, however, especially if the security situation in Mexico deteriorates significantly.

Disagreement over the history of repression in Mexico's border cities included elements of definitional dispute and matters of fact. There was consensus that these cities have occasionally faced episodes of police abuse and incidents of serious human rights abuses by the police or the army. Whether this was sufficient to constitute significant repression, and whether such incidents were in any way systematic, was disputed. One respondent asserted that the acts of the VDTOs were a form of repression, and another argued that the failure of local, state, and federal governments to respond to the crisis of violence against women should be characterized as a form of repression. Another respondent asserted that the government is currently trying to repress the large portions of the population that are part of or are aligned with the DTOs; that respondent labeled this "laudable repression" but repression nonetheless.

Regarding the perception of legitimacy of the government by the governed, many respondents made comments that indicated that they were individually conflicted about this point. It appears that the lack of consensus on this factor is due more to perceptions of shades of gray in the facts than disagreement about the facts. A strong countervailing argument is that, in the areas controlled by the VDTOs, these groups constitute the only authority, and so that authority is de facto legitimate. One comment effectively captures the ambivalence of many of the participants:

> This is a difficult question. I still believe the majority of the public views the Mexican state as legitimate and is patriotic. I also agree that in contested areas (and in reality elsewhere), the public views government with suspicion and is wary of corruption. Certainly corrupt police and security forces, and human rights abuses, reinforce this. Also, public approval for Calderon has as previously indicated been dropping. But, I don't see the cartels as being

viewed as "legitimate" (as much as some would like to develop that perception).

So, legitimacy, to the extent that it is present, is not unambiguous.[5] Further, in areas where the VDTOs assert control, the authority asserted by those organizations may supersede that of the government, rendering the question of government legitimacy temporarily and locally irrelevant, even if the government is otherwise accorded significant legitimacy. As a reviewer of this monograph pointed out, many areas labor under a form of "dual sovereignty," in which elected governments exist side-by-side with VDTO structures, where "silver or lead?" prevails and mayors owe both their position and their survival to VDTO leadership.

Although consensus was reached regarding the absence of the factor "Bad neighborhood (neighboring country war or civil war in last 5 years)," some of the discussion was interesting and salient to this problem set. While everyone agreed that the Guatemalan civil war has been over for more than five years, panelists pointed out several ways in which Mexico is plagued by "bad neighbors." As one panelist noted, "The United States should be considered a bad neighbor from the standpoint of access to guns and the predominant drug market target for the DTOs." Indeed, if one takes a systems approach to the activities of VDTOs, the U.S. drug market and resulting infusions of cash are critical to the economic foundation of the drug traffic, and the flow of guns south from the United States may fuel the violence. Mexico's southern neighbors also make contributions to the challenge, with cocaine from Colombia, Bolivia, and Peru traversing terrestrial routes through Mexico's southern neighbors, and gangs and dissatisfied military or former military elements from Guatemala sometimes joining or collaborating with the VDTOs. Furthermore, history shows that border porosity in countries engulfed in conflict serves to exacer-

[5] See Consulta Mitofsky, *Confianza en las Instituciones: Evaluación Nacional* [*Confidence in Institutions: A National Assessment*], January 2010, for further examples of the declining legitimacy of Mexican institutions.

bate violence and prolong the conflict.[6] Mexico's large, porous southern border with Guatemala is particularly concerning because it serves as a major route for human trafficking and illegal migration from Central America into Mexico and, in many cases, on to the United States. This discussion serves as an important reminder that the challenges brought by VDTOs are not challenges only for Mexico, do not originate exclusively in Mexico, and are unlikely to be completely resolved solely through action on the part of Mexico.

---

[6] Examples include Algeria, El Salvador, Lebanon, Northern Ireland, and Sudan, among others. See Paul Staniland, "Defeating Transnational Insurgencies: The Best Offense Is a Good Fence," *Washington Quarterly*, Vol. 29, No. 1, Winter 2005–2006.

CHAPTER FIVE

Findings from the Counterinsurgency Scorecard

Overall, we remain agnostic as to whether the current security situation in Mexico should be regarded as a form of insurgency. Instead, without presupposing the answer, we ask to what extent the factors currently present in Mexico make it appear similar to any historical insurgencies. If Mexico is viewed as facing an insurgency (counterfactually or otherwise), how would it compare to historical insurgencies? What, if anything, would such an examination tell us?

Like the Urban Flashpoints Scorecard (see Chapter Four), the COIN Scorecard requires binary scores (1,0) rather than the raw proportions represented by the Delphi exercise means (and presented in Table 3.2). Rounding to consensus scores was done in the same way as for the Urban Flashpoints Scorecard. Specifically, if there was at least 70-percent consensus on a factor, the factor was rounded in the direction of consensus (so, scores of 0.7 or higher were rounded to 1, and scores of 0.3 or lower were rounded to 0). For factors without agreement from at least 70 percent of participants, scores were rounded to 0.5, representing neither present nor absent. The required consensus was not reached for 12 of the 54 COIN Scorecard factors; they were thus rounded to 0.5.

Table 5.1 presents the consensus scores for each of the 54 factors. Note that while the scoring portion of the COIN Scorecard accounts for 15 good and 12 bad factors (for a total of only 27 factors, as listed in Table 2.2), many of them are summary factors that combine two or more subordinate factors to make a single factor. For example, "Forces

Table 5.1
Consensus Scores on the Counterinsurgency Scorecard Portion of the Delphi Exercise

COIN Scorecard	Consensus Rounding
Forces of order and government actions consistent with messages (delivering on promises)	0
Forces of order maintaining credibility with populations in the area of conflict (includes expectation management)	0
Messages/themes coherent with overall security approach	0
Forces of order avoid creating unattainable expectations	0
Themes and messages coordinated across all government agencies in or affecting area of conflict	0
Earnest information operation/psychological operation/strategic communication/messaging effort by government/forces of order	0
Unity of effort/unity of command of forces of order maintained	0
Flow of criminal support across border(s) being significantly decreased or remaining dramatically reduced or largely absent	0
Important external support to criminals being significantly reduced	0
Important internal support to criminals being significantly reduced	0
Criminals' ability to replenish resources being significantly diminished	0
Criminals unable to maintain or grow force size	0
Efforts by forces of order resulting in increased costs for criminal processes	0
Forces of order effectively disrupting criminal recruiting	0
Forces of order effectively disrupting criminal materiel acquisition	0
Forces of order effectively disrupting criminal intelligence	0
Forces of order effectively disrupting criminal financing	0
Government corruption reduced/good governance increased since onset of conflict	0
Government leaders selected in a manner considered just and fair by majority of population in the area of conflict	0.5
Majority of citizens view government as legitimate in the area of conflict	0.5

Table 5.1—Continued

COIN Scorecard	Consensus Rounding
Government providing better governance than criminals in area of conflict	0.5
Forces of order providing or ensuring basic services in areas they control or claim to control	0.5
Government a functional democracy	0.5
Government a partial or transitional democracy	0.5
Free and fair elections held	1
Government respects human rights and allows free press	0
Intelligence adequate to lead to capture of or engagements with criminals on the terms of the forces of order	0
Intelligence adequate to allow forces of order to disrupt criminal processes or operations	0.5
Forces of order of sufficient strength to force criminals to fight as guerrillas	0.5
Government/state is competent	1
Forces of order avoiding excessive collateral damage, disproportionate use of force, or other illegitimate applications of force	0
Forces of order seeking to engage and establish positive relations with population(s) in area of conflict	0
Short-term investments, improvements in infrastructure/development, or property reform in area of conflict	0.5
Majority of population in areas of conflict supports/favors forces of order over the criminals	0.5
Forces of order establishing and then expanding secure areas	0
Forces of order have and use uncontested air dominance	1
Perception of security being created or maintained among populations in areas of conflict	0
Forces of order employing escalating repression	0
Forces of order employing collective punishment	0
Primary forces of order come from outside the country	0

Table 5.1—Continued

COIN Scorecard	Consensus Rounding
Forces of order or government actions contributing to substantial new grievances claimed by the criminals or the population	1
Militias working at cross-purposes with forces of order/government	0
Forces of order resettling/removing civilian populations for population control	0
Forces of order collateral damage perceived by population in area of conflict as worse than criminals'	0
In area of conflict, forces of order perceived as worse than criminals	0.5
Forces of order failing to adapt to changes in adversary strategy, operations, or tactics	0.5
Forces of order engaging in more coercion/intimidation than criminals	0
Criminals individually superior to the forces of order by being either more professional or better motivated	1
Forces of order or allies rely on looting for sustainment	0
Forces of order and government have different goals/level of commitment	1

of order realizing at least two strategic communication factors" includes seven subordinate factors.

Is Mexico Like Historical Insurgencies?

Before we compare the COIN Scorecard summary scores (the 15 good factors minus the 12 bad ones) for Mexico with scores for the decisive phases of completed insurgencies, it is useful to compare the scores on the 54 individual component factors with the scores from the intermediate phases of the 30 historical cases.[1] Because 12 of the 54 elements of the COIN Scorecard did not produce consensus results (the factors scored 0.5), we can compare Mexico's scores with the phases of the

[1] From data reported in Paul, Clarke, and Grill, 2010a.

30 cases on 42 factors. Mexico's current scores are not unlike those of the first phase of the insurgency in Peru (matching on 37 of 42 factors), the first phase of the insurgency in Turkey (matching on 35 of 42), the first phase of the Allied Democratic Forces (ADF in the tables) insurgency in Uganda (37 of 42), the first phase of the insurgency in Rwanda (35 of 42), and the first phase of the insurgency in Nepal (35 of 42).

Although we do not want to make too much of these comparisons, it is interesting to note that, of the 86 phases over the 30 cases in the data set, the five phases that contemporary Mexico most closely resembles are all first phases of an insurgency. Of course, the 30 previously examined cases are all cases of *insurgency*; there is an unknown number of historical cases in which countries experienced similar patterns of factors that resulted in something else (perhaps a different form of unrest, or nothing at all). We did find it interesting that contemporary Mexico looks something like the nascent phase of five historical insurgencies, but does not in any way suggest that Mexico is certainly on a path to insurgency.

The fact that contemporary Mexico is not unlike early phases of historical insurgencies is particularly interesting in light of the contention over whether the actions of the VDTOs should be described as an insurgency. Note that several of the governments in the historical insurgency cases refused to acknowledge that they faced an insurgency in the first phase of their cases. Nascent or early insurgencies were initially treated as the activities of mere criminals or terrorists, and combating them was considered strictly a law-enforcement problem not requiring the attention or participation of the rest of the government or the armed forces. Only once the insurgency was sufficiently robust to pose a much greater threat did these governments begin to behave as if they were actually fighting an insurgency.

Mexico's Counterinsurgency Scorecard Score

Without making a decisive claim about the appropriateness of characterizing the current Mexican security situation as an insurgency, we now consider Mexico relative to the 30 historical insurgencies. The COIN Scorecard assessment makes the (arguably counterfactual) assumption that Mexican drug violence *can* be fairly characterized as an insurgency and that government and security forces' counterdrug efforts can be characterized as counterinsurgency. To be clear, this analogy compares Mexican VDTOs as insurgents with insurgencies worldwide between 1978 and 2008 by placing Mexico's score among the scores of 30 historical cases using input from the Delphi panel.

Table 5.2 presents consensus scores for all factors and subfactors on the COIN Scorecard for the RAND Mexican Security Delphi exercise. Rows beginning with numbers are primary factors (the top level factors listed in Table 2.2); rows beginning with lowercase letters are the subfactors that constitute the primary factors.

Based on this exercise, Mexico's COIN Scorecard score is six good factors/practices minus four bad factors/practices for a net score of +2. However, the scorecard contains a total of eight primary scoring factors for which consensus was lacking and 0.5 was used: six of the 15 good factors and two of the 12 bad factors. Pushing these factors to either presence or absence gives us six good factors ±3 (for range of 3–9), and four bad factors ±2 (for a range of 2–6), for a final summary score with a possible range of –3 to 7 if all the consensus scores were resolved in a minimizing or maximizing way. This range highlights the importance of the discussion of factors for which consensus was lacking, presented later in this chapter.

Mexico in Comparison with 30 Historical Cases of Insurgency

Table 5.3 shows where Mexico's COIN Scorecard scores would place it relative to the 30 insurgencies begun and concluded worldwide between 1978 and 2008. The results of the *Victory Has a Thousand Fathers* study show that cases in which the COIN force prevailed are broadly different from cases in which the COIN force lost, which is the primary reason that the COIN scorecard works so well. Mexico's summary score falls in the gap between the two sets of characteristics

Table 5.2
Mexico's Scores on the Counterinsurgency Scorecard

Good Factors	Concensus Scores		
1. Forces of order realizing at least two strategic communication factors (Score 1 if sum of a through g is at least 2)		0	
a. Forces of order and government actions consistent with messages (delivering on promises) (Score 1 if YES)	0		
b. Forces of order maintaining credibility with populations in the area of conflict (includes expectation management) (Score 1 if YES)	0		
c. Messages/themes coherent with overall security approach (Score 1 if YES)	0		
d. Forces of order avoiding creating unattainable expectations (Score 1 if YES)	0		
e. Themes and messages coordinated for all government agencies in or impacting area of conflict (Score 1 if YES)	0		
f. Earnest information operation/psychological operation/ strategic communication/messaging effort (Score 1 if YES)	0		
g. Unity of effort/unity of command maintained (Score 1 if YES)	0		
2. Forces of order reducing at least three tangible support factors (Score 1 if sum of a through j is at least 3)		0	
a. Flow of criminal support across border(s) being significantly decreased or remaining dramatically reduced or largely absent (Score 1 if YES)	0		
b. Important external support to criminals being significantly reduced (Score 1 if YES)	0		
c. Important internal support to criminals being significantly reduced (Score 1 if YES)	0		
d. Criminals' ability to replenish resources being significantly diminished (Score 1 if YES)	0		
e. Criminals unable to maintain or grow force size (Score 1 if YES)	0		
f. Forces of order efforts resulting in increased costs for criminal processes (Score 1 if YES)	1		
g. Forces of order effectively disrupting criminal recruiting (Score 1 if YES)	0		

Table 5.2—Continued

Good Factors	Concensus Scores		
h. Forces of order effectively disrupting criminal materiel acquisition (Score 1 if YES)	0		
i. Forces of order effectively disrupting criminal intelligence (Score 1 if YES)	0		
j. Forces of order effectively disrupting criminal finance (Score 1 if YES)	0		
3. Government realizing at least two government legitimacy factors (Score 1 if sum of a through e is at least 2)		0.5	
a. Government corruption reduced/good governance increased since onset of conflict (Score 1 if YES)	0		
b. Government leaders selected in a manner considered just and fair by majority of population in the area of conflict (Score 1 if YES)	0.5		
c. Majority of citizens view government as legitimate in the area of conflict (Score 1 if YES)	0.5		
d. Government providing better governance than criminals in area of conflict (Score 1 if YES)	0.5		
e. Forces of order providing or ensuring basic services in areas they control or claim to control (Score 1 if YES)	0.5		
4. Government realizing at least one democracy factor (Score 1 if sum of a through d is at least 1)		1	
a. Government a functional democracy (Score 1 if YES)	0.5		
b. Government a partial or transitional democracy (Score 1 if YES)	0.5		
c. Free and fair elections held (Score 1 if YES)	1		
d. Government respects human rights and allows free press (Score 1 if YES)	0		
5. Forces of order realizing at least one intelligence factor (Score 1 if sum of a and b is at least 1)		0.5	
a. Intelligence adequate to support kill/capture or engagements on forces of order's terms (Score 1 if YES)	0		
b. Intelligence adequate to allow forces of order to disrupt criminal processes or operations (Score 1 if YES)	0.5		

Table 5.2—Continued

Good Factors	Concensus Scores		
6. Forces of order of sufficient strength to force criminals to fight as guerrillas (Score 1 if YES)		0.5	
7. Government/state competent (Score 1 if YES)		1	
8. Forces of order avoiding excessive collateral damage, disproportionate use of force, or other illegitimate applications of force (Score 1 if YES)		0	
9. Forces of order seeking to engage and establish positive relations with population(s) in area of conflict (Score 1 if YES)		0	
10. Short-term investments, Improvements in infrastructure/ development, or property reform in area of conflict controlled or claimed by the forces of order (Score 1 if YES)		0.5	
11. Majority of population in areas of conflict supports/favors forces of order (Score 1 if YES)		0.5	
12. Forces of order establishing and then expanding secure areas (Score 1 if YES)		0	
13. Forces of order have and use uncontested air dominance (Score 1 if YES)		1	
14. Forces of order providing or ensuring basic services in areas they controlled or claimed to control (Score 1 if YES)		0.5	
15. Perception of security being created or maintained among populations in areas forces of order claims to control (Score 1 if YES)		0	
Total positive score (Sum of 1–15)			6

Bad Factors	Concensus Scores		
1. Forces of order using both collective punishment and escalating repression (Score 1 if sum of a and b is at least 1)		0	
a. Forces of order employing escalating repression (Score 1 if YES)	0		
b. Collective punishment employed by forces of order (Score 1 if YES)	0		
2. Primary forces of order come from outside the country (Score 1 if YES)		0	
3. Forces of order or government actions contributing to substantial new grievances claimed by the criminals (Score 1 if YES)		1	

Table 5.2—Continued

Bad Factors		Concensus Scores	
4. Militias working at cross-purposes with forces of order/ government (Score 1 if YES)		0	
5. Forces of order resettling/removing civilian populations for population control (Score 1 if YES)		0	
6. Forces of order collateral damage perceived by population in area of conflict as worse than criminals' (Score 1 if YES)		0	
7. In area of conflict, forces of order perceived as worse than criminals (Score 1 if YES)		0.5	
8. Forces of order failing to adapt to changes in adversary strategy, operations, or tactics (Score 1 if YES)		0.5	
9. Forces of order engaging in more coercion/intimidation than criminals (Score 1 if YES)		0	
10. Criminal force individually superior to the forces of order by being either more professional or better motivated (Score 1 if YES)		1	
11. Forces of order or allies rely on looting for sustainment (Score 1 if YES)		0	
12. Forces of order and government have different goals/level of commitment (Score 1 if YES)		1	
Total negative score (Sum of 1–12)			4
Final score (good minus bad):			2

that are common in the historical data. On good factors, the consensus score for Mexico is +6, which is lower than that of any of the COIN winners but better than that of any of the COIN losers. With regard to bad factors, historical winners and losers partially overlap—and again, Mexico's score is right in the space of overlap: Mexico's score of 4 is better than the worst COIN winner's score but is more typical of the better-scoring losers. Mexico's summary score of +2 again falls in the empirical gap between winners (+5 and higher) and losers (0 and below). If the threat from VDTOs in Mexico were best characterized as an insurgency, and if the current scores accurately represent the decisive phase, the lessons of insurgencies over the past 30 years are equivocal on the outcome.

However, it remains an open question whether the current situation in Mexico can be appropriately characterized as an insurgency or whether it will become one. Even if insurgency is an appropriate perspective through which to view the current (or future) conflict with the VDTOs, such an insurgency is currently in its earliest phase or phases, not the terminal or decisive phase (the phase considered in the case-level scores for the 30 historical cases). If the security situation in Mexico is or becomes an insurgency, the Mexican government and security forces will have ample opportunity to develop and implement COIN efforts, thus changing the scores on the scorecard. (Most of the 30 historical cases realized significant changes in factors present or absent through the different phases of each case.) One of the key findings of the earlier study was that "poor beginnings do not necessarily lead to poor ends"; in fully six of the eight cases won by the COIN force, the insurgents had the upper hand in an earlier phase but the COIN force improved its balance on the scorecard in its favor and ultimately prevailed.[2]

Counterinsurgency Scorecard Factors for Which Consensus Was Lacking and Other Items of Interest from the Delphi Discussion

Twelve of the 54 individual factors on the COIN Scorecard, and eight of the 27 resulting superordinate primary scoring factors, were not the subject of consensus among the Delphi panelists. The 12 factors for which consensus was not achieved were as follows:

- Government leaders selected in a manner considered just and fair by majority of population in the area of conflict
- Majority of citizens view government as legitimate in the area of conflict

[2] See Paul, Clarke, and Grill, 2010b, p. xxiii.

Table 5.3
Where Mexico Would Fit Among 30 Insurgencies Worldwide, 1978–2008

Case	Good Factors (of 15)	Bad Factors (of 12)	Good – Bad Factors	Outcome
Afghanistan (post-Soviet)	0	10	–10	Loss
Somalia	1	10	–9	Loss
Chechnya I	2	10	–8	Loss
Rwanda	2	10	–8	Loss
Zaire (anti-Mobutu)	0	8	–8	Loss
Nicaragua (Somoza)	0	8	–8	Loss
Sudan (SPLA)	2	9	–7	Loss
Kosovo	1	8	–7	Loss
Afghanistan (anti-Soviet)	1	7	–6	Loss
Papua New Guinea	3	9	–6	Loss
Burundi	2	8	–6	Loss
Bosnia	1	6	–5	Loss
Moldova	2	6	–4	Loss
Georgia/Abkhazia	1	5	–4	Loss
Liberia	3	7	–4	Loss
Afghanistan (Taliban)		6	–4	Loss
Nagorno-Karabakh		4	–3	Loss
DR Congo (anti-Kabila)		4	–3	Loss
Tajikistan		5	–3	Loss
Kampuchea	1	3	–2	Loss
Nepal	3	5	–2	
Nicaragua (Contras)	4	4	0	
Mexico (VDTOs)	6	4	+2	
Croatia	8	3	+5	
Turkey (PKK)	11	5	+6	
Uganda (ADF)	8	0	+8	Win
Algeria (GIA)	9	1	+8	Win
El Salvador	12	2	+10	Win
Peru	13	2	+11	Win
Senegal	13	0	+13	Win
Sierra Leone	14	1	+13	Win

At 4, Mexico is better than the worst-scoring winner but also close to many losers.

At +2, Mexico is in the empirical gap between winners and losers over the past 30 years.

At 6, Mexico is better than any loser but worse than any winner.

- Government providing better governance than criminals in area of conflict
- Forces of order providing or ensuring basic services in areas they control or claim to control
- Government a functional democracy
- Government a partial or transitional democracy
- Intelligence adequate to allow forces of order to disrupt criminal processes or operations
- Forces of order of sufficient strength to force criminals to fight as guerillas
- Short-term investments, improvements in infrastructure/ development, or property reform in area of conflict
- Majority of population in area of conflict supports/favors forces of order over the criminals
- In area of conflict, forces of order perceived as worse than criminals
- Forces of order failing to adapt to changes in adversary strategy, operations, or tactics.

Because of these disagreements, the discussion was particularly robust. In what follows, we share some of the details of the disagreement and interesting points raised or observations made over the course of the discussion.

The first several factors for which consensus was lacking have to do with government legitimacy. This was also a factor sparking controversy in the discussion of the Urban Flashpoints Scorecard (see Chapter Four).

In the discussion surrounding the selection of leaders, government legitimacy, and the provision of governance and services, two issues drove those in dissent to contest the presence of these positive factors. The first was corruption. No one disputed that there is a high level of penetration of the government and the law enforcement forces by the VDTOs, or that the government—especially at the local and state levels—suffers from rampant corruption (Chapter Four explained the perception of state governors as "new viceroys"). The area where there was disagreement concerned whether the level of corruption was sufficient to undermine the legitimacy of the government or the fairness of the electoral and government appointment processes. The lack of consensus on these factors showcases this disagreement.

The second issue driving dissenting views regarding government legitimacy, governance, and provision of services was the existence of so-called "zones of impunity" in Mexico. In these areas, there is no government presence, and to the extent that services or governance are provided, it is either by, or under sufferance of, the VDTOs. As one clearly conflicted panelist noted,

> Not sure where to go with this. I certainly don't believe the cartels provide better governance. I also believe there are significant areas in Mexico where the government is absent and state capacity is weak.

Another area of dispute among the Delphi participants was the maturity of Mexico's democracy. Here, the disagreement was more about definitions than it was about facts. Everyone agreed that Mexico's emergence from one-party rule was an important step toward a more mature democracy, and everyone agreed that corruption in the government undermines the ability of democracy to be meaningfully realized at certain levels of the polity. According to one participant,

> In regions of the country you have to get permission to run for office or you can get killed by corrupt governmental or cartel forces. Those undesirable candidates get killed while campaigning, get forced out of running, or get killed after they get in office.

While some may argue that Mexico does not meet the minimal requirements of a transitional democracy, there was consensus among the Delphi participants that Mexico *is* a transitional democracy. The disagreement among participants was more about the threshold required to move from transitional democracy to full or mature democracy, and consensus on that threshold was not reached.

Also leading to interesting discussion were disagreements about the extent to which the government and the forces of order were preferred over the VDTOs and the relative perception of the forces of order versus the criminals. There was significant disagreement here, and the facts clearly differ by location. Some participants pointed out that, in certain locales, VDTOs account for the only functioning part of the economy, and any governance and services available are provided by these organizations or under their sufferance. In these locales, the police and the army are viewed as a threat to safety, stability, and the local economy. Others pointed out the existence of human rights complaints against the military and the police, asserting that "there is little to no support for the military/police."

Others indicated that the forces of order are usually preferred over the VDTOs but that such support is often lukewarm at best. As one participant noted,

> The Mexican public opinion polling I have seen indicates very low levels of public support for police forces, and significantly higher (though declining) levels of public support for military forces, but almost no measurable support for criminal gangs.

Equivocation was typical in the responses, especially when considering "worst-case" instances; arguably, in this case, the lack of consensus represents something that is genuinely neither present nor absent. As one panelist observed, "I've concluded that in many areas, both the criminals and forces of order are looked upon with disdain." Even if on balance the forces of order are preferable to the VDTOs, this is clearly a situation that the forces of order need to improve upon.

The discussion of several factors highlighted different perceptions of the local government and police in contrast with perceptions of the federal government, the federal police, and the armed forces. Panelists indicated that the local police in many areas are viewed as corrupt or inept, along with the local (and sometimes state) government. The federal government and federal forces are held in distinctly higher (though not perfect) regard.

Corruption remained the single biggest (and most often mentioned) concern raised across the board. Corruption was mentioned as having an adverse impact in a substantial number of COIN Scorecard factor areas, including corruption itself, grievances, democracy and legitimacy, governance, provision of services, intelligence, and support for and perception of the forces of order.[3]

---

[3] This view and concern is not limited to the panel; see, for example, A. W. Goudie and David Stasavage, "A Framework for the Analysis of Corruption," *Crime, Law, and Social Change*, Vol. 29, Nos. 2–3, March 1998.

CHAPTER SIX

Findings from the Defense Sector Assessment Rating Tool Scorecard

Participants in the Delphi exercise were asked to use the DSART Scorecard to score Mexico on its core capabilities related to counternarcotics, counterterrorism or COIN, and border and maritime security along the following scale:

1. *very low:* entirely lacking
2. *low:* beginning to develop
3. *neither low nor high:* minimal but functioning
4. *high:* functional but room for development
5. *very high:* strong and no major improvement needed.

Overall, the Delphi panel scored all of Mexico's capabilities across the three security issues at 3.18 or below, indicating that Mexico's core capabilities related to these three security issues are minimal but functioning at best and entirely lacking at worst. On average, the panel's score for capabilities in each of the three security issues was *low.* In this chapter, we briefly present the findings from the DSART Scorecard portion of the RAND Mexican Security Delphi exercise.

Assessment of Mexico's Counternarcotics Capabilities

Participants in the exercise were asked to score Mexico's core counternarcotics capabilities on the 1–5 scale. Table 6.1 illustrates the capabilities that the panelists were asked to score and the panel's final scores, ranked from high to low.

Table 6.1
Assessment of Mexico's Counternarcotics Capabilities

Defense Sector Assessment Rating Tool (DSART) Scorecard Section	Mean
Assessment of Counternarcotics Capabilities	
Police, prosecute, and incarcerate drug traffickers	1.91
Maintain law and order (public safety)	1.91
Integrate military and law-enforcement operational support	1.82
Maintain border and coastal security	2.55
Collect intelligence on narcotics traffickers	2.36
Control corruption in counternarcotics operations	1.27
Establish drug eradication and interdiction programs	2.45
Develop rapid and mobile reaction capabilities based on real-time intelligence	2.18
Train civilians and military forces in counternarcotics operations	2.09
Control roadways, airspace, and waterways	2.45
Average	2.10

The Delphi panel rated all of Mexico's counternarcotics capabilities as either *low* or *very low*. The scores for Mexico's counternarcotics capabilities range from a high score of 2.55 for the capability to maintain border and coastal security to a low score of 1.27 for the capability to control corruption in counternarcotics operations. The average score across all the capabilities related to counternarcotics is 2.10.

Assessment of Mexico's Counterterrorism and Counterinsurgency Capabilities

Participants were also asked to score Mexico's core counterterrorism and COIN capabilities on the same 1–5 scale. Table 6.2 lists the capabilities that the panelists were asked to score and the panel's final scores, ranked from high to low.

Table 6.2
Assessment of Mexico's Counterterrorism and Counterinsurgency Capabilities

Defense Sector Assessment Rating Tool (DSART) Scorecard Section	Mean
Assessment of Counterterrorism or Counterinsurgency Capabilities	
Maintain security throughout the country	2.36
Collect and analyze intelligence	2.45
Provide policing and law enforcement	1.91
Protect critical infrastructure	3.18
Carry out military surveillance and interdiction	2.45
Integrate strategic communication	1.82
Hold territory and control roadways, waterways, and airspace	3.00
Contribute to the design and delivery of an overall integrated government strategy and operations	2.09
Control corruption in government counterterrorism and counterinsurgency operations	1.64
Disrupt financing by terrorist or insurgent groups from within or outside the country	1.82
Deny support to terrorist or insurgent groups from domestic populations or from outside the country	1.91
Average	2.24

The Delphi panel rated all of Mexico's counterterrorism and COIN capabilities as *neither low nor high* and below. The scores ranged from a high of 3.18 for the capability to protect critical infrastructure to a low of 1.64 for the capability to control corruption in government counterterrorism and COIN operations. The average score across all the capabilities related to counterterrorism and COIN is 2.24.

Assessment of Mexico's Border and Maritime Security Capabilities

Finally, participants in the RAND Mexico Security Delphi exercise were asked to score Mexico's core border and maritime capabilities on the 1–5 scale. Table 6.3 presents the capabilities that the panelists were asked to score and the panel's final scores, ranked from high to low.

The panelists rated all of Mexico's border and maritime capabilities as either *low* or *very low*. The scores for Mexico's border and maritime capabilities ranged from a high score of 2.64 for the capability to coordinate with neighboring states and the international community on border security to a low score of 1.45 for the capability to control corruption in border and maritime operations. The average score across all the capabilities related to border and maritime capabilities is 2.08.

Table 6.3
Assessment of Mexico's Border and Maritime Security Capabilities

Defense Sector Assessment Rating Tool (DSART) Scorecard Section	Mean
Assessment of Border and Maritime Security Capabilities	
Patrol and secure land and maritime borders	2.36
Track people and goods entering and leaving the country	2.18
Control corruption in border and maritime security operations	1.45
Coordinate with neighboring states and international community on border security	2.64
Collect intelligence and conduct border surveillance	2.09
Train military forces on border and maritime security while border security tasks are transitioned to nonmilitary border management agency	1.73
Average	2.08

Overall Findings

The scores indicate that the panel's impression is that Mexico's security sector has limited capabilities to counter drug trafficking, terrorism and insurgency, and porous land and maritime borders. The panel consistently ranked the capability to control corruption as the weakest capability across the three security issues and a barrier to other capabilities. This was also captured in the discussion, with one participant stating, "I think that the Mexican government is able to collect quite a bit of information on DTOs but corruption often hinders the actions taken on the basis of that intelligence." Another participant said that "accounts of rampant corruption abound. In my view, corruption in the forces of order are the single biggest barrier to effectively opposing the DTOs." Overall, the discussion during this portion of the Delphi exercise indicated that there was a surprising amount of consensus on the capabilities that the panelists were asked to score.

During the discussion of Mexico's counterterrorism and COIN capabilities, several panelists expressed skepticism regarding the relevance of applying the terms "terrorism" and "insurgency" to the current situation in Mexico. For instance, one panelist said, "I don't see anything that suggests that the Mexican government is currently focusing on terrorist organizations; rather, the current messaging appears to be on labeling local groups as terrorists." According to another panelist, "What insurgent groups exist are very isolated and weak, and only threaten local stability. I don't know that this is an issue unless you want to classify organized crime as terrorists or insurgents. I'm not prepared to do that yet."

When asked about Mexico's ability to disrupt financing by terrorist or insurgent groups from within or outside the country, one participant responded that "this is perhaps the greatest shortcoming of the Mexican strategy and plan to fight narcoterrorism. There is really no evidence that Mexico is capable of doing this without the support and leadership of American intelligence."

CHAPTER SEVEN

Conclusions and Suggestions for Further Research

The findings from this research effort highlight consistencies across the three assessment scorecards and common conclusions among the expert panelists in the RAND Mexican Security Delphi exercise.

Conclusions

First, according to the expert panelists' responses on the Urban Flashpoints Scorecard, Mexican border cities are at risk for continued urban unrest, specifically the depredations of the VDTOs. Several very concerning factors work in combination to sustain this form of unrest: the preexistence of the VDTOs, unmet economic expectations and high unemployment, the presence of a demographic "youth bulge," a high level of corruption in government and law enforcement, and low rule of law.

Second, according to the COIN Scorecard results, if the current security situation in Mexico were appropriately characterized as an insurgency, it appears that Mexico is in the gap between two modes of historical insurgencies; cases with characteristics corresponding to one of the modes were won by the government, and those with the other set of modal characteristics were government losses. Whether or not Mexico's struggle with VDTOs deserves to be characterized as an insurgency, Mexico would do well to seek more of the characteristics of the modal victors.

Third, in a detailed comparison with the various phases of 30 historical insurgencies, Mexico has the most in common with the first phase of several cases, suggesting that insurgency is one of the possible future trajectories for Mexico. If its current struggle with the VDTOs is not unlike the first phase of several historical insurgencies, Mexico would do well to avoid making the mistakes common to the early phases, including the historical propensity to fail to acknowledge the presence of an insurgency until it is fairly robust.

Fourth, based on the DSART results, Mexico's policing capabilities continue to be weak. The Delphi panel's impression was that some of Mexico's weakest capabilities are the ability to police, prosecute, and incarcerate drug traffickers; the ability to maintain law and order; and the ability to integrate military and law-enforcement operational support. Unless Mexico's policing capabilities are strengthened, it will continue to struggle to carry out these critical functions.

Fifth, Mexico faces growing challenges in the areas of legitimacy, governance, provision of services, and positive regard for the government and security forces in the areas contested or occupied by VDTOs. The fact that the expert panel was split on many of these issues suggests that these areas are not complete losses for the Mexican government, but they are in jeopardy. The fact that these issues came up in a scorecard designed to assess vulnerability to unrest and progress against insurgency suggests that they are very important and worth seeking to improve.

Sixth, the challenges Mexico faces from VDTOs are not Mexico's alone. Both its northern and southern neighbors contribute to the problem as part of the extended economy of the VDTOs and will be instrumental in finding and implementing durable solutions.

Finally, in all three scorecard phases of the exercise and associated discussion, corruption was the single biggest (and most often mentioned) concern. Corruption undermines defense-sector reform, efforts to combat VDTOs, and the legitimacy and support offered to the government and security forces by Mexico's citizens. The adverse impact of corruption and the criticality of making improvements with regard to corruption cannot be overstated.

For Future Research

This application of existing RAND research to Mexico's security challenges has raised at least as many questions as it has answered. Here, we briefly suggest additional research in this area that could be particularly productive.

Further Comparison

The challenges posed by VDTOs raise important questions about effective efforts to oppose such groups in other times and places. The question remains, What are the appropriate comparison groups?

For reasons discussed earlier, we agree that traditional insurgencies might not be the most fruitful comparison group. However, we believe that comparative research on any (or all) of the following would be beneficial:

- *Resource insurgencies:* These are cases in which insurgents did not seek to win control of the state or establish their own government but simply sought to eliminate state interference with their exploitation of natural resources (be it diamonds, drugs, timber, or other enterprises). Cases might include Afghanistan, Angola, Burma, Colombia, Lebanon, Liberia, Nigeria, Peru, Sierra Leone, Tajikistan, and Yugoslavia.
- *Warlordism or ungoverned territories:* These cases are similar to resource insurgencies, but the rejection of state authority was not sufficiently opposed by the state to earn the insurgency label. Cases of warlordism might include Afghanistan, Angola, Burma, Kampuchea, Chad, Chechnya, Colombia, Democratic Republic of Congo, Georgia, Kurdistan, Lebanon, Liberia, Mozambique, Peru, Philippines, Sierra Leone, Somalia, Tajikistan, and Serbia. Instances of ungoverned spaces of possible interest include the Pakistani-Afghan border region, the Ferghana Valley, the Arabian Peninsula, the Sulawesi-Mindanao Arc, the East Africa corridor, West Africa, the North Caucasus, the Colombia-Venezuela border, and the Guatemala-Chiapas border.

- *Efforts to combat organized crime:* Whether or not they have become something more, Mexican VDTOs are certainly an instance of organized crime. A study of such efforts might ask, When organized crime has been actively opposed in other places and times, what has proven effective and what pitfalls have been revealed? Possible cases of interest include Albania, Bulgaria, Brazil, Colombia, Romania, Russia/Ukraine, Sicily, Turkey, Tanzania, and Thailand.
- *Alternative paths from situations like the early phases of some insurgencies:* In Chapter Five, we note that contemporary Mexico shares significant similarities with the early phases of several historical insurgencies examined as part of the previous research effort. It is also possible that these same characteristics are shared by other countries, in other times and places, and did not lead to full-blown insurgencies. Research on this topic could employ case-control matching, a method often used in medical research in which a patient with a condition (in this case, insurgency) is paired with a control individual who is as similar as possible to the afflicted patient, excepting that they do not have the condition of interest. Examples of situations similar to some early-phase insurgencies that did not develop in that direction include the race riots of the 1970s in the United States, intercommunal violence in Singapore in the 1950s, and the Baader-Meinhof campaign in Germany in the 1970s, for example.

A Closer Examination of Mexico

The Delphi panel was unable to reach consensus on a number of issues (five Urban Flashpoints factors and 12 COIN Scorecard factors). These factors are of potential interest for further research not so much from a desire to get the scorecards "right" as to explore the complexity and the nuance in the Mexican security situation that prevented the panel from agreeing. Do these factors as worded really not apply in Mexico? Do they mean something else in that context, and is that meaning interesting or relevant? What are the security implications of the complexities noted by the Delphi panelists in the rich discussion?

While not all of the disputed factors are of equal interest, several merit further attention and investigation of the specifics in Mexico—and perhaps comparative research regarding similar situations elsewhere:

- the nature of homelands and contested homelands inside Mexico
- the relationship between the Mexican military and the civilian government
- the legitimacy of the Mexican government (and the electoral process) at all levels in different parts of Mexico and for different polities
- the competing provision of governance and services by the Mexican government and the VDTOs
- the character, quality, and extent of Mexican democracy at the various levels of government
- variations in the behavior of VDTOs and various government security forces in different parts of the country, as well as perceptions of those behaviors by different constituencies
- the relative capabilities of various security forces and various VDTOs.

A Systems Perspective

VDTOs are complex, adaptive organizations. Thus, there is a need for complex organizational and economic analysis to understand the systems that underlie these enterprises. Such analysis would begin with a logic model and identify inputs and outputs to the larger system, including the enumeration of activities (the full supply chain of drug production and trafficking, for example), as well as ancillary activities (e.g., kidnapping, various forms of violence) and their relationships to other enterprises. This basic model could be elaborated to consider input and output flows, numbers and types of personnel involved, types of locations and facilities required, and so on. Ideally, such analysis would help identify bottlenecks or weaknesses in the overall system—bottlenecks that could be further tightened or weaknesses that could be otherwise exploited. Such a systems analysis might also be useful for predicting "balloon" implications of pressure on certain parts of the system (the balloon metaphor often emerges when pressure is put on one organization or location and criminal enterprise reduces where pressure is applied but expands elsewhere), or it could better identify the implications of systemic vacancy chains. Such a systems perspective would also provide a useful analytic lens for proposals related to the decriminalization or legalization of drugs, showing where certain elements of the VDTO economy would see their monetary values enhanced and their associated risks increased because these elements are illegal.[1]

---

[1] For example, see Beau Kilmer, Jonathan P. Caulkins, Rosalie Liccardo Pacula, Robert J. MacCoun, and Peter H. Reuter, *Altered State? Assessing How Marijuana Legalization in California Could Influence Marijuana Consumption and Public Budgets*, Santa Monica, Calif.: RAND Corporation, OP-315-RC, 2010, for an analysis of the impact of marijuana legalization in California.

References

Archibald, Randal C., "Mexican Leader Pushes Police Overhaul," *New York Times*, October 7, 2010. As of July 1, 2011:
http://www.nytimes.com/2010/10/08/world/americas/08mexico.html

Beittel, June S., *Mexico's Drug Trafficking Organizations: Source and Scope of the Rising Violence*, Washington, D.C.: Congressional Research Service, January 7, 2011.

Brown, Bernice B., *Delphi Process: A Methodology Used for the Elicitation of Opinions of Experts*, Santa Monica, Calif.: RAND Corporation, P-3925, 1968. As of July 1, 2011:
http://www.rand.org/pubs/papers/P3925.html

Bunker, Robert J., "Strategic Threat: Narcos and Narcotics Overview," *Small Wars and Insurgencies*, Vol. 21, No. 1, 2010, pp. 8–29.

Castillo, E. Eduardo, "Mexico Decries U.S. Official's Reference to 'Form of Insurgency' by Drug Gangs," *Washington Post*, February 10, 2011.

Caulkins, Jonathan P., Peter Reuter, Martin Y. Iguchi, and James Chiesa, *How Goes the "War on Drugs"? An Assessment of U.S. Drug Problems and Policy*, Santa Monica, Calif.: RAND Corporation, OP-121-DPRC, 2005. As of July 1, 2011:
http://www.rand.org/pubs/occasional_papers/OP121.html

"Ciudad Juarez Sees 40 Killed in Violent Weekend," BBC News, February 21, 2011. As of July 1, 2011:
http://www.bbc.co.uk/news/world-latin-america-12521696

Consulta Mitofsky, *Confianza en las Instituciones: Evaluación Nacional* [*Confidence in Institutions: A National Assessment*], January 2010.

"Drug Killings Make 2010 Deadliest Year for Mexico Border City," Associated Press, January 1, 2011. As of July 1, 2011:
http://www.foxnews.com/world/2011/01/01/mexico-border-city-record-drug-killings

Entous, Adam, and Nathan Hodge, "U.S. Sees Heightened Threat in Mexico," *Wall Street Journal*, September 10, 2010, p. A8.

Finnegan, William, "Silver or Lead," *New Yorker*, Vol. 86, No. 15, May 31, 2010, p. 39. As of July 1, 2011:
http://www.newyorker.com/reporting/2010/05/31/100531fa_fact_finnegan

Friman, H. Richard, "Drug Markets and the Selective Use of Violence," *Crime, Law, and Social Change*, Vol. 52, No. 3, 2009, pp. 285–295.

Goudie, A. W., and David Stasavage, "A Framework for the Analysis of Corruption," *Crime, Law, and Social Change*, Vol. 29, Nos. 2–3, March 1998, pp. 113–159.

Goldstone, Jack A., *Revolution and Rebellion in the Early Modern World*, Berkeley, Calif.: University of California Press, 1991.

Gompert, David C., Olga Oliker, Brooke Stearns Lawson, Keith Crane, and K. Jack Riley, *Making Liberia Safe: Transformation of the National Security Sector*, Santa Monica, Calif.: RAND Corporation, MG-529-OSD, 2007. As of July 1, 2011:
http://www.rand.org/pubs/monographs/MG529.html

Iraq Body Count, *Documented Civilian Deaths from Violence*, data as of March 22, 2011. As of March 22, 2011:
http://www.iraqbodycount.org/database/

Jones, Seth G., and Arturo Muñoz, *Afghanistan's Local War: Building Local Defense Forces*, Santa Monica, Calif.: RAND Corporation, MG-1002-MCIA, 2010. As of July 1, 2011:
http://www.rand.org/pubs/monographs/MG1002.html

Kan, Paul Rexton, and Phil Williams, "Afterword: Criminal Violence in Mexico—A Dissenting Analysis," *Small Wars and Insurgencies*, Vol. 21, No. 1, March 2010, pp. 218–231.

Killebrew, Bob, and Jennifer Bernal, *Crime Wars: Gangs, Cartels and U.S. National Security*, Washington, D.C.: Center for New American Security, September 2010.

Kilmer, Beau, Jonathan P. Caulkins, Brittany M. Bond, and Peter H. Reuter, *Reducing Drug Trafficking Revenues and Violence in Mexico: Would Legalizing Marijuana in California Help?* Santa Monica, Calif.: RAND Corporation, OP-325-RC, 2010. As of July 1, 2011:
http://www.rand.org/pubs/occasional_papers/OP325.html

Kilmer, Beau, Jonathan P. Caulkins, Rosalie Liccardo Pacula, Robert J. MacCoun, and Peter H. Reuter, *Altered State? Assessing How Marijuana Legalization in California Could Influence Marijuana Consumption and Public Budgets*, Santa Monica, Calif.: RAND Corporation, OP-315-RC, 2010. As of July 1, 2011:
http://www.rand.org/pubs/occasional_papers/OP315.html

Kurtzman, Joel, "Mexico's Instability Is a Real Problem: Don't Discount the Possibility of a Failed State Next Door," *Wall Street Journal*, January 16, 2009.

Mann, Michael, *The Sources of Social Power*, Vol. 2: *The Rise of Classes and Nation-States, 1760–1914*, Cambridge, UK: Cambridge University Press, 1993.

Marquis, Jefferson P., Jennifer D. P. Moroney, Justin Beck, Derek Eaton, Scott Hiromoto, David R. Howell, Janet Lewis, Charlotte Lynch, Michael J. Neumann, and Cathryn Quantic Thurston, *Developing an Army Strategy for Building Partner Capacity for Stability Operations*, Santa Monica, Calif.: RAND Corporation, MG-942-A, 2010. As of July 1, 2011:
http://www.rand.org/pubs/monographs/MG942.html

"Mexico Town's Police Force After Attack: We Quit," Associated Press, November 2, 2010. As of July 1, 2011:
http://www.cbsnews.com/stories/2010/10/26/world/main6993871.shtml

"Mexico's Drug War: Number of Dead Passes 30,000," BBC News, December 16, 2010. As of July 1, 2011:
http://www.bbc.co.uk/news/world-latin-america-12012425

Moroney, Jennifer D. P., and Joe Hogler, with Benjamin Bahney, Kim Cragin, David R. Howell, Charlotte Lynch, and Rebecca Zimmerman, *Building Partner Capacity to Combat Weapons of Mass Destruction*, Santa Monica, Calif.: RAND Corporation, MG-783-DTRA, 2009. As of July 1, 2011:
http://www.rand.org/pubs/monographs/MG783.html

Moroney, Jennifer D. P., Joe Hogler, Jefferson P. Marquis, Christopher Paul, John E. Peters, and Beth Grill, *Developing an Assessment Framework for U.S. Air Force Building Partnerships Programs*, Santa Monica, Calif.: RAND Corporation, MG-868-AF, 2010. As of July 1, 2011:
http://www.rand.org/pubs/monographs/MG868.html

O'Brien, Sean P., "Anticipating the Good, the Bad, and the Ugly: An Early Warning Approach to Conflict and Instability Analysis," *Journal of Conflict Resolution*, Vol. 46, No. 6, December 2002, pp. 791–811.

Oliker, Olga, Keith Crane, Audra K. Grant, Terrence K. Kelly, Andrew Rathmell, and David Brannan, *U.S. Policy Options for Iraq: A Reassessment*, Santa Monica, Calif.: RAND Corporation, MG-613-AF, 2007. As of July 1, 2011:
http://www.rand.org/pubs/monographs/MG613.html

"Organized Crime in Mexico," *STRATFOR*, March 11, 2008.

Paul, Christopher, Colin P. Clarke, and Beth Grill, *Victory Has a Thousand Fathers: Detailed Counterinsurgency Case Studies*, Santa Monica, Calif.: RAND Corporation, MG-964/1-OSD, 2010a. As of July 1, 2011:
http://www.rand.org/pubs/monographs/MG964z1.html

———, *Victory Has a Thousand Fathers: Sources of Success in Counterinsurgency*, Santa Monica, Calif.: RAND Corporation, MG-964-OSD, 2010b. As of July 1, 2011:
http://www.rand.org/pubs/monographs/MG964.html

Paul, Christopher, Russell W. Glenn, Beth Grill, Megan P. McKernan, Barbara Raymond, Matt Stafford, and Horacio R. Trujillo, "Identifying Urban Flashpoints: A Delphi Derived Model for Scoring Cities' Vulnerability to Large Scale Unrest," *Studies in Conflict and Terrorism*, Vol. 31, No. 11, 2008, pp. 1032–1051.

Reyes, Alfonso, "Plan Mexico? Towards an Integrated Approach in the War on Drugs," *Small Wars Journal*, September 14, 2010.

Schaefer, Agnes Gereben, Benjamin Bahney, and K. Jack Riley, *Security in Mexico: Implications for U.S. Policy Options*, Santa Monica, Calif.: RAND Corporation, MG-876-RC, 2009. As of July 1, 2011:
http://www.rand.org/pubs/monographs/MG876.html

Schaefer, Agnes Gereben, Lynn E. Davis, Ely Ratner, Molly Dunigan, Jeremiah Goulka, Heather Peterson, and K. Jack Riley, *Developing a Defense Sector Assessment Rating Tool*, Santa Monica, Calif.: RAND Corporation, TR-864-OSD, 2010. As of July 1, 2011:
http://www.rand.org/pubs/technical_reports/TR864.html

Snyder, Richard, and Angelica Duran-Martinez, "Does Illegality Breed Violence? Drug Trafficking and State-Sponsored Protection Rackets," *Crime, Law, and Social Change*, Vol. 52, No. 3, 2009, pp. 253–273

Staniland, Paul, "Defeating Transnational Insurgencies: The Best Offense Is a Good Fence," *Washington Quarterly*, Vol. 29, No. 1, Winter 2005–2006, pp. 21–40.

Sullivan, John P., and Adam Elkus, "Plazas for Profit: Mexico's Criminal Insurgency," *Small Wars Journal*, 2009. As of July 1, 2011:
http://smallwarsjournal.com/blog/journal/docs-temp/232-sullivan.pdf

Treverton, Gregory F., *Making Policy in the Shadow of the Future*, Santa Monica, Calif.: RAND Corporation, OP-298-RC, 2010. As of July 1, 2011:
http://www.rand.org/pubs/occasional_papers/OP298.html

U.S. Agency for International Development, U.S. Department of Defense, and U.S. Department of State, *Security Sector Reform*, February 2009.

U.S. Department of State, Bureau of International Narcotics and Law Enforcement Affairs, *2010 International Narcotics Control Strategy Report,* Vol. 1: *Drug and Chemical Control*, Washington, D.C., March 2010. As of July 1, 2011:
http://www.state.gov/p/inl/rls/nrcrpt/2010/vol1

———, *2011 International Narcotics Control Strategy Report 2011,* Vol. 1: *Drug and Chemical Control,* Washington, D.C., March 2011. As of July 1, 2011: http://www.state.gov/p/inl/rls/nrcrpt/2011/vol1

Walsh, Mark, "Mexican Town's Cops Quit After Colleagues Beheaded," Associated Press, January 28, 2011. As of July 1, 2011: http://www.elpasotimes.com/ci_17226671

Wilkinson, Tracy, and Ken Ellingwood, "Mexico's Army's Failures Hamper Drug War," *Los Angeles Times,* December 29, 2010. As of July 1, 2011: http://articles.latimes.com/2010/dec/29/world/la-fg-mexico-army-20101230

Wong, Carolyn, *How Will the e-Explosion Affect How We Do Research? Phase I: The E-DEL+I Proof-of-Concept Exercise,* Santa Monica, Calif.: RAND Corporation, DB-399-RC, 2003. As of July 1, 2011: http://www.rand.org/pubs/documented_briefings/DB399.html

Zuckerman, Leo, "Los Nuevos Virreyes" ["The New Viceroys"], *Proceso,* July 13, 2003.